FUN
AND
GAMES

100 Sport-Related Activities for Ages 5-16

**Anthony Dowson,
BSc (Hons), PGCE**
Loughborough Grammar School

Keith E.J. Morris, BA (Hons)
Grass Roots

Human Kinetics

Library of Congress Cataloging-in-Publication Data

Dowson, Anthony, 1975-
  Fun and games : 100 sport-related activities for ages 5-16 / Anthony Dowson, Keith E.J. Morris.
    p. cm.
  Includes bibliographical references.
  ISBN 0-7360-5438-3 (soft cover)
  1. Sports for children. 2. Games. 3. Physical fitness for children. I. Morris, Keith E.J., 1974- II. Title.
  GV709.2.D69 2005
  796'.083--dc22

                                                                                    2004016501

ISBN: 0-7360-5438-3

Acquisitions Editor: Bonnie Pettifor; **Developmental Editors:** Diane Evans and Amy Stahl; **Assis-
tant Editors:** Derek Campbell and Bethany Bentley; **Copyeditor:** Sheena Cleland; **Proofreader:** Sue
Fetters; **Graphic Designer:** Fred Starbird; **Graphic Artist:** Tara Welsch; **Photo Manager:** Kareema
McLendon; **Cover Designer:** Keith Blomberg; **Photographer (cover):** © Media Bakery; **Photographer
(interior):** © Human Kinetics, unless otherwise noted. Photo on page 65 © Media Bakery. Photo on
page 89 © SportsChrome; **Art Managers:** Kelly Hendren and Kareema McLendon; **Illustrator:** Craig
Newsom; **Printer:** Versa Press

Printed in the United States of America   10   9   8   7   6   5   4   3   2   1

Human Kinetics
Web site: www.HumanKinetics.com

United States: Human Kinetics
P.O. Box 5076
Champaign, IL 61825-5076
800-747-4457
e-mail: humank@hkusa.com

Canada: Human Kinetics
475 Devonshire Road Unit 100
Windsor, ON N8Y 2L5
800-465-7301 (in Canada only)
e-mail: orders@hkcanada.com

Europe: Human Kinetics
107 Bradford Road
Stanningley
Leeds LS28 6AT, United Kingdom
+44 (0) 113 255 5665
e-mail: hk@hkeurope.com

Australia: Human Kinetics
57A Price Avenue
Lower Mitcham, South Australia 5062
08 8277 1555
e-mail: liaw@hkaustralia.com

New Zealand: Human Kinetics
Division of Sports Distributors NZ Ltd.
P.O. Box 300 226 Albany
North Shore City
Auckland
0064 9 448 1207
e-mail: blairc@hknewz.com

Contents

Preface

With over 20 years' coaching and teaching experience we have realised that children's sporting encounters need to be *fun*. Children love to play games, and if they are involved in entertaining activities, it helps them in the following ways:

- It keeps them focused and on task.
- It helps them to form positive attitudes towards physical activity.
- It helps to keep them more active.

Over the years we have developed an array of activities and games which we use every day when teaching children. We have also received many requests for a resource of fun activities and games for children from a number of teachers and coaches. Therefore this book aims to create such a resource by compiling a collection of the best activities. The underlying premise of this book is that all activities have been chosen because children enjoy them. This book is predominantly aimed at teachers, coaches and sport leaders. However, anyone who has the responsibility of organising activities for young people can use an assortment of ideas from the book.

The book contains a range of warm-up ideas, games, skill practices and sport-specific activities to enthuse and motivate youngsters. All activities are fully inclusive, involving each participant throughout. We find that with greater involvement, participants enjoy themselves more and are more receptive to learning.

It is important that children develop skills in sport and physical education so they make progress in relation to their peers. This should lead to greater levels of self-confidence and self-esteem, which are associated with improving in sport. Through using the ideas in this book, you will be able to develop children's skills as they participate in fun and enjoyable activities. We guarantee that children will leave the session having had fun and wanting to come back for more.

Many activities require minimal equipment and are easy to set up. They can be used as part of a one-off session, or included in longer-term planning. The format for the book is simple; text is kept to a minimum and extensive use of illustrations helps to keep it user-friendly. The book is broken down into eight chapters containing a total of 100 activities. In the first chapter are 34 *multi-sport* activities. The subsequent seven chapters deal with specific sports: basketball (or netball), cricket (striking and fielding), hockey, parachute games, rugby, soccer and tennis (badminton). Although an activity may appear in one of the sport-specific sections, many can be modified for use in other sports. Even the activities in the multi-sport chapter can be modified for use in other sports. This means that although the title states there are 100 activities contained in the book, effectively there are many more.

We believe that with an increase in childhood obesity there is a need for children to lead healthier lifestyles. For some children, this involves being physically active more often. We hope that if you use these activities regularly with your groups, it can help in the development of positive attitudes to physical education and sport.

Acknowledgements

To Mum and Marie-Anne
Thanks for all your love and support. You are amazing!
Thanks to Major League Soccer Camps for shaping my coaching philosophy and 'lifting me beyond my vision of capability'.
Tony

So many thanks to Mum, Dad and Amy, my motivation for everything.
Keith

This book is also dedicated to those who have helped in the creation, from the proposal that seemed so far away to the final production you have in your hands. To Steve Williams, Diane Evans, Dave Ryan and Steph Howard: We couldn't have got there without you. You are very much appreciated.

To Bob Holmes, who has helped us greatly over the years and been an inspiration in our careers.

How to Use This Book

Each chapter contains a brief introduction of the types of activities included. This introductory section also includes important safety recommendations for each group of activities, so it is vital that you read this section before embarking on an activity.

In the sport-specific chapters we have tried to include games that anyone could implement. The majority of games do not require you to be a trained physical education teacher or have specific coaching qualifications to play them with a group. However, if you are not coaching or teaching regularly, we advise you to enrol on relevant coaching award courses in order to gain these qualifications. This should help you to develop your participants' skill levels in addition to providing them with these fun activities.

Game Finder

A breakdown of all the activities is found in the game finder on pages xi-xxi. This lists the activities alphabetically and gives the page number(s) so you can quickly locate each one. The game finder also gives recommended age ranges for each activity, which should help you decide whether it is suitable for the participants you are leading. The game finder also includes skills and fitness components developed by each activity. Some activities can be adapted for use in other specific sports and, if so, the game finder lists these.

Game Format

Each activity is written in easy-to-understand and set-up sections. The sections include:

- Ages
- Equipment
- Game
- Safety Tips

- Advice
- Variations

Ages

A number of the activities can be used when instructing children of any age. Some are more suited to a particular age group, but the recommendations given should enable you to plan your sessions effectively for a variety of participants. Note that the ages given are only recommendations. You may find that the participants you instruct enjoy a particular activity even if they do not fall within the suggested age range. For example, when coaching adults and tutoring coach education courses, we have used a number of the activities and found that children are not the only ones to have fun with them! An indication of suitable age ranges is given at the start of each game.

Equipment

This section lists the minimum equipment needed to carry out an activity. If you do not have enough equipment you should consult the Variations section of each game as there may be an alternative way of playing which requires less equipment.

Game

The Game section explains how to set up and run each activity effectively. Some games are played in small groups, whereas others can be 'mass' activities performed by all. Normally group sizes are listed so you can identify the numbers needed to carry out the activity effectively. Group numbers are only suggestions. You may be able to modify an activity to suit your group.

Use the information in the Game section to explain how to play the activity. We have provided an illustration where necessary to help you organise the activity successfully. For some activities we recommend sizes for playing area(s). For other activities we do not specify size of playing area(s) as this depends on the age, ability and numbers in your group. The size of the area should allow safe involvement and provide adequate opportunities for success. An example of this is Beat the Fielder in the Cricket, Striking and Fielding chapter (see page 66). The distance between the two teams for the average 5-year-old participant would be considerably less than the distance needed for the average 16-year-old participant, but we have used this game with both age groups and they have both enjoyed playing it. In some cases you may need to use common sense to determine the size of an area needed for an activity. If you have less experience, first start the activity and monitor how effectively it is running. Then if the activity is not working well, stop the activity and change the size of the area(s) before continuing.

Safety Tips

Participation in sport carries an inherent risk of injury, but instructors can minimise this by adequate control of the group and by not exposing participants to unnecessary dangers. The tips included in this section provide guidance to ensure activities are carried out safely and effectively. Tips include

- instructions you give
- things to be mindful of
- rule-related information.

Advice

Under this heading information is given to help ensure the activity runs smoothly. Advice may include tips on how to best explain the activity, how to group the participants or other related issues.

Variations

The Variations section provides alternative ways of running the activity. The section may suggest a slightly different way of playing, or ways to change the level of difficulty. Sometimes an activity can be carried out with more or fewer participants and the information here should help you decide if you can adapt one to suit the numbers you have. When activities can be adapted for other sports, these are listed here.

Warming Up and Cooling Down

It is important to start each session by warming up. A warm-up prepares the body and mind for the activity ahead and can also prevent injury. It is vital that older children are taken through a good warm-up to prevent muscle injuries such as tears and strains. The need for a warm-up to prevent injury in younger children is probably less important but they should be taught good habits as early as possible. For further information on warm-up and cool-down exercises, see Harris and Elbourn (2002).

A progressive warm-up should include the following:

- Pulse-raising activities should start at a low to moderate intensity. The activities should be progressive and aim to increase muscle temperature. This initial part should last for a minimum of 3 to 5 minutes depending on the environmental temperature. Examples include jogging and sidestepping.

- Mobility exercises should be used to warm up and 'loosen' the joints. Examples include shoulder and ankle circling.
- Stretching exercises should be incorporated to improve the range of movement at a joint. These can include static or dynamic stretches. Examples of static stretches could be hamstring and calf stretches, whereas dynamic stretches involve moving a body part slowly through a full range of motion. Examples of dynamic stretches include leg swinging and heel flicks.

A number of the activities found in the book are suitable for use as part of a progressive warm-up. Most involve pulse-raising activities, so mobility and stretching exercises should be incorporated into them. As many of the activities involve ballistic movements and/or sprinting it is also important that participants cool down to help recover after playing them.

Reference

Harris, J. and Elbourn, J. 2002. *Warming Up and Cooling Down.* Champaign, IL: Human Kinetics.

Game Finder

Name of game	Page number	Age group suitable for	Equipment	Sports suitable for	Skills needed/ developed	Fitness components needed/ developed
CHAPTER 1—MULTI-SPORT GAMES						
Arches	2	5 to 13 yrs	Bibs and cones	N/A	Running, chasing, dodging	Agility, balance, reaction time, speed
Back to Back	3	5 to 13 yrs	None	Soccer	Running	Agility, balance, reaction time, speed
Bench Relay	5	5 to 16 yrs	Benches and cones	N/A	Running	Reaction time, power, speed
Body Parts (Ball)	6	5 to 16 yrs	Any type of sport ball	Any ball sport	Decision making	Reaction time
Body Parts (Numbers)	7	5 to 10 yrs	Cones	Gymnastics	Decision making, running	Agility, coordination, reaction time
Capture the Ball	8	8 to 16 yrs	Bibs, cones and sport balls	Basketball, rugby, soccer	Running, chasing, dodging	Agility, balance, coordination, endurance, reaction time, speed
Catch and Release	11	5 to 13 yrs	Cones and bibs	Soccer	Running, chasing, dodging	Agility, balance, reaction time, speed
Chasers	12	5 to 13 yrs	Cones and bibs	N/A	Running, chasing, dodging	Agility, balance, reaction time, speed
Circle Hold	13	5 to 13 yrs	None	N/A	Decision making	Agility, balance, reaction time
Copy Command	14	5 to 10 yrs	Cones	Basketball, hockey, soccer	Running	Agility, reaction time
Do This, Do That	15	5 to 13 yrs	None	N/A	Decision making	Reaction time
Freeze	16	5 to 13 yrs	Cones	Basketball, hockey, soccer	Running, chasing, dodging	Agility, balance, reaction time, speed

(continued)

Name of game	Page number	Age group suitable for	Equipment	Sports suitable for	Skills needed/ developed	Fitness components needed/ developed
CHAPTER 1—(CONTINUED)						
Group Of	17	5 to 16 yrs	Cones	N/A	Decision making, running	Endurance, reaction time, speed
Hills and Hollows	18	5 to 13 yrs	Cones	N/A	Running	Agility, balance, reaction time, speed
Hit but Not Out	19	5 to 16 yrs	Bibs, benches and sponge balls	N/A	Dodging, throwing	Agility, balance, coordination, power, reaction time
Hoop Defender	21	8 to 16 yrs	Bibs, hoops and sponge balls	N/A	Running, dodging, throwing	Agility, balance, coordination, endurance, reaction time, speed
Jailbreak	22	5 to 13 yrs	Bibs and cones	N/A	Running, chasing, dodging	Agility, balance, reaction time, speed
Linda's Game	23	5 to 13 yrs	Beanbags or sport balls	N/A	Running	Balance, reaction time, speed
Line Tag	25	5 to 13 yrs	Bibs	N/A	Running, chasing	Agility, balance, reaction time, speed
Mass Invasion	26	8 to 16 yrs	Beanbags, bibs, coloured balls, cones and hoops	N/A	Running, chasing, dodging	Agility, balance, coordination, endurance, reaction time, speed
Opposites	28	5 to 10 yrs	Cones	N/A	Decision making, running, jumping	Agility, reaction time
Partner Run	29	5 to 16 yrs	Cones	Basketball, hockey, soccer	Any skills chosen	Agility, endurance, speed, coordination

Name of game	Page number	Age group suitable for	Equipment	Sports suitable for	Skills needed/ developed	Fitness components needed/ developed
Put Out, Pick Up Relay	31	5 to 13 yrs	Beanbags, cones and hoops	N/A	Running, throwing	Speed
Roller Ball	32	5 to 16 yrs	Balls and cones	Basketball, hockey, soccer	Running, rolling a ball, receiving skills	Coordination, endurance, reaction time
Shuttles	34	5 to 13 yrs	Cones	Basketball, hockey, soccer	Running, any skills chosen by instructor	Reaction time, speed
Stars and Stripes	35	5 to 13 yrs	Cones	Hockey, soccer	Decision making, running	Reaction time, speed
Sticky Toffee	37	5 to 13 yrs	Bibs and cones	Basketball, soccer	Running, chasing, communi- cation skills, dodging	Agility, balance, reaction time, speed
Tails	38	5 to 13 yrs	Bibs and cones	N/A	Running, chasing, dodging	Agility, balance, reaction time, speed
Team Drop	39	11 to 16 yrs	Balls and cones	Volleyball, soccer	Hitting/ passing, throwing	Agility, balance, reaction time
Team Take	41	5 to 13 yrs	Cones, hoops and sport balls	Hockey, basketball, soccer	Running	Speed
Thawed Out	43	5 to 13 yrs	Cones	Soccer	Running, chasing, dodging	Agility, balance, reaction time, speed
Total Relay	44	5 to 13 yrs	Cones	Basketball, hockey, soccer	Running, any skills chosen	Coordination, endurance, speed
Touch and Go!	46	5 to 10 yrs	Cones	Soccer	Decision making, running	Agility, coordination, reaction time
Trio Dodge	47	5 to 13 yrs	None	N/A	Chasing, dodging	Agility, balance, coordination, reaction time

(continued)

Name of game	Page number	Age group suitable for	Equipment	Sports suitable for	Skills needed/ developed	Fitness components needed/ developed
CHAPTER 2—BASKETBALL AND NETBALL GAMES						
Follow the Leader	50	5 to 16 yrs	Basketballs	Basketball, almost all other activities	Any skills chosen by participants	Dependant on actions chosen by participants
Hit It	51	5 to 13 yrs	Basketballs, large cones	Basketball, netball, soccer	Passing, receiving	Coordination, power
Knockout	53	5 to 16 yrs	Basketballs, bibs, cones	Basketball, hockey, soccer	Dribbling, defending	Agility, balance, coordination, reaction time, speed
One-Hand Dribble	54	5 to 16 yrs	Basketballs, cones	Basketball, hockey, soccer	Dribbling, defending	Agility, balance, coordination, reaction time, speed
Partner Shoot	55	5 to 16 yrs	Basketballs, baskets, stopwatch	Basketball, netball	Shooting, rebounding, passing, receiving	Agility, balance, coordination, power, speed
Rebound	56	11 to 16 yrs	Basketballs, backboard	Basketball	Rebounding	Coordination, power, strength
Sharpshooter	58	8 to 16 yrs	Basketballs, baskets	Basketball, netball	Shooting, rebounding	Agility, balance, coordination, reaction time
Stealer Basketball	60	5 to 16 yrs	Basketballs, cones	Basketball, hockey, soccer	Dribbling, defending	Agility, balance, coordination, reaction time, speed
Team Shoot	61	5 to 16 yrs	Basketballs, baskets, cones	Basketball, netball	Shooting, rebounding, passing, receiving	Agility, balance, coordination, power, speed
Twenty-One	62	8 to 16 yrs	Basketballs, baskets	Basketball, netball	Shooting, rebounding	Agility, coordination, reaction time, speed

Name of game	Page number	Age group suitable for	Equipment	Sports suitable for	Skills needed/ developed	Fitness components needed/ developed
CHAPTER 3—CRICKET, STRIKING AND FIELDING GAMES						
Beat the Fielder	66	5 to 16 yrs	Cones and tennis balls	Cricket, rounders, baseball, softball, soccer	Catching, fielding, throwing	Agility, balance, coordination, power, reaction time
Circuit Cricket	68	5 to 16 yrs	Cricket bats, tennis balls and wickets	Cricket, rounders, baseball, softball	Batting, catching, fielding, throwing, wicketkeeping	Agility, balance, coordination, power, reaction time, speed
Drop, Bounce, Hit	70	5 to 16 yrs	Cones, tennis balls and wickets	Cricket, rounders, baseball, softball	Batting, catching, throwing, fielding	Agility, balance, coordination, power, reaction time
Line and Length	72	8 to 16 yrs	Hoops (or chalk), tennis balls and wickets	Cricket	Bowling, wicketkeeping	Coordination, power, reaction time
Non-Stop Batting	74	5 to 16 yrs	Cricket bats, cones, tennis balls and wickets	Cricket and soccer	Batting, catching, fielding, throwing, wicketkeeping	Agility, balance, coordination, power, reaction time, speed
Play or Not	76	8 to 16 yrs	Cricket bats, cones, tennis balls and wickets	Cricket	Batting (decision making), bowling, wicketkeeping	Balance, coordination, power, reaction time
Score the Single	79	5 to 16 yrs	Cricket bats, tennis balls and wickets	Cricket, rounders, baseball, softball	Batting, catching, fielding, throwing, wicketkeeping	Agility, balance, coordination, power, reaction time, speed
Take Away Five	81	11 to 16 yrs	Cricket bats, tennis balls and wickets	Cricket	Batting, catching, fielding, throwing, wicketkeeping	Agility, balance, coordination, power, reaction time, speed

(continued)

Name of game	Page number	Age group suitable for	Equipment	Sports suitable for	Skills needed/developed	Fitness components needed/developed
CHAPTER 3—(CONTINUED)						
Throw and Back Up	83	8 to 16 yrs	Cones, cricket bats, tennis balls and wickets	Cricket	Batting, bowling, fielding, throwing	Agility, balance, coordination, power, reaction time, speed
Tip and Run	86	5 to 16 yrs	Cricket bats, tennis balls and wickets	Cricket	Batting, catching, fielding, throwing, wicketkeeping	Agility, balance, coordination, power, reaction time, speed
CHAPTER 4—HOCKEY GAMES						
Best out of Nine	90	8 to 16 yrs	Cones, goals, goalkeeper's equipment, hockey balls and hockey sticks	Hockey	Passing, shooting, defending skills	Balance, coordination, power, reaction time, speed
Flip and Turn	92	8 to 13 yrs	Cones, hockey balls, hockey sticks and mini-hurdles	Hockey, basketball and soccer	Dribbling	Balance, coordination, endurance
Horses and Jockeys	93	5 to 16 yrs	Hockey balls and hockey sticks	Hockey, basketball and soccer	Dribbling	Balance, reaction time, speed
Score to Run Out	95	8 to 13 yrs	Cones, goals, hockey balls and hockey sticks	Hockey and soccer	Hitting, shooting, passing, teamwork	Agility, balance, coordination, power, reaction time, speed
Speed Shot	98	8 to 16 yrs	Goals, hockey balls and hockey sticks	Hockey	Shooting	Balance, coordination, power
Traffic Control	100	5 to 10 yrs	Cones, hockey balls and hockey sticks	Hockey, basketball and soccer	Dribbling	Agility, balance, coordination, reaction time, speed

Name of game	Page number	Age group suitable for	Equipment	Sports suitable for	Skills needed/ developed	Fitness components needed/ developed
Winner Stays On	101	14 to 16 yrs	Bibs, cones, goalkeeper's equipment, goals, hockey balls and hockey sticks	Hockey	Attacking and defending skills	Agility, balance, coordination, endurance, power, reaction time, speed
Zigzag Pass	103	5 to 16 yrs	Cones, hockey balls and hockey sticks	Hockey, basketball, cricket, netball, rugby and soccer	Passing, receiving	Balance, coordination, reaction time, speed
Zone Attack	105	8 to 16 yrs	Bibs, cones, hockey balls and hockey sticks	Hockey	Attacking and defending skills	Agility, balance, coordination, endurance, power, reaction time, speed

CHAPTER 5—PARACHUTE GAMES

Name of game	Page number	Age group suitable for	Equipment	Sports suitable for	Skills needed/ developed	Fitness components needed/ developed
Ball Flick	110	5 to 10 yrs	Football or volleyball and a parachute	Parachute	Teamwork	Coordination, power
Carousel	111	5 to 10 yrs	Parachute	Parachute	Running	Balance, coordination, speed
Cat and Mouse	112	5 to 10 yrs	Parachute	Parachute	Chasing, dodging	Agility, balance, reaction time
Colours	114	5 to 10 yrs	Parachute	Parachute	Running	Reaction time, speed
Dome	115	5 to 10 yrs	Parachute	Parachute	Teamwork	Coordination, power, reaction time
Kites	116	5 to 10 yrs	Parachute	Parachute	Teamwork	Coordination, power
The Cooler	117	5 to 10 yrs	Parachute	Parachute	Teamwork	Coordination, power

(continued)

Name of game	Page number	Age group suitable for	Equipment	Sports suitable for	Skills needed/ developed	Fitness components needed/ developed
CHAPTER 6—RUGBY GAMES						
Attacking Run	122	8 to 16 yrs	Cones and rugby balls	Rugby, basketball, hockey, soccer	Attacking, defending	Agility, balance, reaction time, speed
Catch Tag	124	5 to 16 yrs	Cones and rugby balls	Rugby, basketball, netball, cricket	Passing, receiving, dodging	Agility, balance, coordination, reaction time, speed
Don't Let Them Drop	126	8 to 16 yrs	Rugby balls	Rugby, basketball, netball, cricket	Passing, receiving	Coordination, reaction time
Draw and Pass	129	8 to 16 yrs	Cones and rugby balls	Rugby, basketball, hockey, soccer	Passing, receiving, attacking, defending	Agility, balance, coordination, reaction time, speed
How Fast Can You Pass?	132	5 to 10 yrs	Rugby balls	Rugby, cricket, basketball, netball	Passing, receiving	Coordination, speed
Keep Away	133	5 to 16 yrs	Cones and rugby balls	Rugby, basketball, netball, cricket	Passing, receiving, dodging	Agility, balance, coordination, reaction time, speed
Numbers Attack	135	5 to 16 yrs	Bibs, cones and rugby balls	Rugby, basketball, hockey, soccer	Passing, receiving, attacking, defending	Agility, balance, coordination, reaction time, speed
Removable Rugby	137	8 to 16 yrs	Bibs, cones and rugby balls	Rugby, basketball, hockey, soccer	Passing, receiving, attacking, defending	Agility, balance, coordination, reaction time, speed
Ruck, Maul or Pass	139	11 to 16 yrs	Cones and rugby balls	Rugby (union only)	Tackling, team play, passing, receiving, attacking, defending	Agility, balance, coordination, power, reaction time, speed, strength

Name of game	Page number	Age group suitable for	Equipment	Sports suitable for	Skills needed/ developed	Fitness components needed/ developed
Try	141	5 to 16 yrs	Cones and rugby balls	Rugby, basketball, hockey, soccer	Passing, receiving, attacking, defending	Agility, reaction time, speed

CHAPTER 7—SOCCER GAMES

Name of game	Page number	Age group suitable for	Equipment	Sports suitable for	Skills needed/ developed	Fitness components needed/ developed
Admiral's Inspection	144	5 to 7 yrs	Cones and soccer balls	Soccer, basketball, hockey	Dribbling	Agility, balance, coordination, reaction time, speed
Doctor, Doctor	145	5 to 13 yrs	Bibs, cones and soccer balls	Soccer	Dribbling, passing, dodging	Agility, balance, coordination, endurance, reaction time, speed
Dodge the Pass	148	5 to 10 yrs	Cones and soccer balls	Soccer	Passing, dodging	Agility, balance, coordination, reaction time, speed
Dribble Chase	150	5 to 16 yrs	Cones and soccer balls	Soccer	Dribbling, passing, dodging	Agility, balance, coordination, reaction time, speed
Dribble Gates	151	5 to 13 yrs	Cones and soccer balls	Soccer, basketball, hockey	Dribbling	Agility, balance, coordination, reaction time, speed
Dribble Pass	153	5 to 13 yrs	Cones and soccer balls	Soccer	Dribbling, passing, dodging	Agility, balance, coordination, reaction time, speed
Head Catch	154	5 to 10 yrs	Soccer balls	Soccer	Heading, catching	Balance, coordination, reaction time
Rapid Fire	156	8 to 16 yrs	Cones, goals and soccer balls	Soccer	Shooting, passing, goalkeeping	Agility, coordination, endurance, power

(continued)

Name of game	Page number	Age group suitable for	Equipment	Sports suitable for	Skills needed/ developed	Fitness components needed/ developed
CHAPTER 7—(CONTINUED)						
Shift It	159	5 to 10 yrs	Cones and soccer balls	Soccer, hockey	Passing, control	Agility, balance, coordination, reaction time, speed
Two Touch	161	8 to 16 yrs	Cones and soccer balls	Soccer, hockey	Passing, control	Agility, balance, coordination, reaction time, speed
CHAPTER 8—TENNIS AND BADMINTON GAMES						
Catch to Score	166	8 to 16 yrs	Chalk, tennis balls, courts and rackets	Tennis, badminton	Ground strokes or volleying	Agility, balance, coordination, reaction time, speed
Champ of the Court	168	8 to 16 yrs	Chalk, tennis balls, courts and rackets	Tennis, badminton, table tennis	All shots	Agility, balance, coordination, power, reaction time, speed
Conveyor Belt	170	5 to 10 yrs	Cones, tennis balls and rackets	Tennis, badminton, table tennis	Coordination of racket	Balance, coordination, speed
Learn the Lines	171	5 to 13 yrs	Tennis courts	Tennis, badminton	Footwork	Agility, reaction time, speed
Line Rally	174	8 to 13 yrs	Tennis balls, courts and rackets	Tennis	Footwork, basic hitting skills	Agility, balance, coordination, reaction time
Net Champ	175	8 to 16 yrs	Tennis balls, courts and rackets	Tennis, badminton	Volleying, net play	Agility, balance, coordination, reaction time, speed
React	176	5 to 16 yrs	Tennis balls	Tennis, basketball, netball, rugby	Catching, footwork	Reaction time, speed
Shadow Play	178	5 to 16 yrs	Tennis courts and rackets	Tennis, badminton	Any simulated shots	Balance, coordination, reaction time

Name of game	Page number	Age group suitable for	Equipment	Sports suitable for	Skills needed/ developed	Fitness components needed/ developed
Team Rally	179	8 to 16 yrs	Tennis balls, courts and rackets	Tennis, badminton, table tennis	Ground strokes or volleying	Agility, balance, coordination, power, reaction time, speed
Three in a Row	182	8 to 16 yrs	Tennis balls, courts and rackets	Tennis, badminton, table tennis	All shots	Agility, balance, coordination, power, reaction time, speed

Multi-Sport
Games

The activities in this chapter are generic activities. Most of the activities involve every participant in the group working on the same task. A number of activities can be used as part of a progressive warm-up. The activities are fun-based and require minimal equipment. Also included are

- games which children have recreated in the playground,
- variations on tag games and
- team games.

Most activities are vigorous involving running and dodging to encourage activity.

Arches

● EQUIPMENT

One bib per five or six participants, cones.

● GAME

Cone out your working area and ask the participants to form pairs. Choose some of the pairs to become chasers and ask each chaser to put a bib on. There should be one pair of chasers for every five or six pairs. The chasers run after the other pairs trying to tag them. All participants run around holding hands or wrists with their partner. If either one of a pair being chased is tagged, they are both 'caught' and form an arch (figure 1.1). Other pairs being chased can 'free' those caught by running through the arch. Continue the game for a set time or until the chasers tag all of the other pairs.

Figure 1.1

Safety Tips

▸ Warn participants to be careful of collisions.

▸ Communication skills are required within the pairs so they both run in the same direction.

● ADVICE

- Change the chasers regularly.
- During the game, you can help free participants or reduce the number of chasers if you think too many are static (i.e., in the arch position).
- If participants let go of each other's hands while being chased they must form the arch position. Encourage them to keep hold of their partner tightly.

● VARIATIONS

- **Easier/Harder:** Variations of the arched shape could be created using other body parts (e.g., in seated position putting feet together).
- **Harder:** Arches are stuck until two other pairs go under.

Back to Back  AGES 5-13

● EQUIPMENT

None.

● GAME

Separate the participants into pairs and number them one and two. Participants sit on the floor back to back with their legs straight (figure 1.2a). Shout 'one round'. All number ones get up and race around their partners (figure 1.2b), with the winner being the first person to get back to the starting position.

Figure 1.2a

Figure 1.2b

Then shout 'two round' for number two to run around their partner. You can then call out for either participant to race around their partner in random order. Each participant has a few goes. Other instructions such as the following can be added:

- One or two over—participants leapfrog over their partners, who adopt a crouched position.
- One or two under—participants crawl under their partners, who adopt a press-up position.
- One or two on—participants jump onto their partner's back in a 'piggyback' position.

After each activity the participants should return to a back-to-back position on the floor.

Safety Tips

▸ You should match participants for size and weight if you are using the 'one on' or 'two on' command.

ADVICE

- Time commands so that the participants are active for as long as possible but are able to complete the action before the next command.
- For younger participants, add one new command at a time.

VARIATIONS

- **Easier:** For younger participants make 'over' easier by making the 'frog' curl up in a ball on the floor.
- **Easier/Harder:** Can the participants think of other instructions? For example, 'one hop round', where number one would hop around their partner.
- **Harder:** Participants perform the actions twice or more on command (e.g., go round their partner twice).
- **Large groups:** Adapt the game for groups of three.
- **Sport-specific:** The game can be adapted to specific sports, such as soccer, by dribbling a ball. In this case, do not use the 'on' command.

Bench Relay

 EQUIPMENT

One bench per six participants, cones.

 GAME

Line up the benches beside each other 3 to 5 m apart and arrange the participants into teams of six with each team sitting on a bench. Number the teams. Place a cone 15 to 20 m in front of each bench.

Instruct the participants that if you call out their team's number they all have to stand up as quickly as possible. Call out another number and the team standing up has to sit down while the next team called has to stand (figure 1.3).

All the participants must move at the same time to stand up or sit down. If a participant from a team moves too slowly to react or not everyone in the team stands up or sits down at the same time, then that team all run around the cone placed in front of their team while the rest of the teams start counting down the time (i.e., '10 . . . 9 . . . 8 . . .'). If they don't all get back in time they have to do a fun challenge.

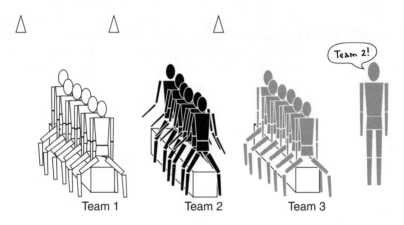

Team 1   Team 2   Team 3

Figure 1.3

Safety Tips

▶ Inform the participants to be careful when they return to the benches.

✸ ADVICE

- Time the shuttle so that the participants work hard but are able to make it.
- If some participants are reacting too slowly, then put them at the back of their bench so that they have more team-mates to copy.

✸ VARIATIONS

- **Easier/Harder:** Instead of doing a shuttle, the participants can run around their own bench or all the benches as a different challenge.
- **Game variation:** Make up a scoring system to add competition.

Body Parts (Ball) AGES 5-16

✸ EQUIPMENT

One sport ball of any type between two.

✸ GAME

Arrange the participants into pairs. Instruct each participant to face their partner with a ball on the floor between them. Shout out a part of the body. Participants place their hands on that part of their own body. If at any time you shout 'ball' the participants compete against their partner to grab the ball first, but you should call out a number of body parts before 'ball' (e.g., 'knees, feet, shoulder, ball'). Whoever gets the ball is awarded a point. For very young participants call out simple body parts such as 'right foot', 'knees', 'eyes' and so on. For older participants, call out muscle groups and bones to make it more difficult.

> **Safety Tips**
>
> ▶ Make sure the participants are standing far enough apart that they do not clash heads when they reach down for the ball.

✸ ADVICE

- Instruct participants to keep their legs straight and stand up tall so that they are not crouching ready to grab the ball.

- Add a cone 5 m away from each participant and add an occasional jog or sprint round the cone to increase the intensity.
- If both participants grab the ball at the same time award a point each to avoid conflicts between them (unless it is a rugby practice in which case you can coach about 'ripping' the ball from someone). Change the participants' partners regularly to maintain motivation.

VARIATIONS

- **Large groups:** This game can be played in a group of three.

Body Parts (Numbers)   AGES 5-10

EQUIPMENT

Cones.

GAME

This activity is good for use as part of a progressive warm-up. Cone out your working area. Participants run around the area in different directions, slowly building up speed.

Once the participants are moving around, call out a number.

The participants must place that number of body parts in contact with the floor. The participants hold their position so you can assess whether they have the right number of body parts touching the floor.

The participants then get up and move around again, until a new number is called out. Figure 1.4 shows a participant attempting to place two body parts on the floor whereas figure 1.5 shows an attempt at five body parts.

Figure 1.4   Figure 1.5

> ### Safety Tips
>
> ▶ Ensure the participants have sufficient space in which to move to minimise the risk of collisions.
>
> ▶ Warn participants to be careful of collisions.

✸ ADVICE

- Keep encouraging the participants.
- Encourage the participants not to repeat any positions if the same number is called out more than once.
- Class the hand as one body part.

✸ VARIATIONS

- **Harder:** Only allow participants to have one hand or foot in contact with the floor each time you call out a number.
- **Harder:** Play in groups of two or three. Participants must make contact with each other to make a combined shape.
- **Sport-specific:** Adapted for gymnastics, the activity can be useful in a session on balances.

Capture the Ball   AGES 8-16

✸ EQUIPMENT

One sport ball each, cones in three different colours, one bib between two in one colour.

✸ GAME

This is a sporting variation of the game Capture the Flag. It can be complicated to explain, so try to include all of the following points in your explanation.

Set up the area using coloured cones as shown in figure 1.6. Separate the participants into two teams, with one team wearing the bibs. Each team stands in one half of the playing area. Cones should be used to mark out a halfway line, a 'jail' (7 × 7 m) in each half and a 'store' (7 × 7 m) in each half, where the balls are kept. Half of the balls should be placed in each store. The objective of the game is for players to defend their own team's balls while also trying to 'capture' balls from the opposing team.

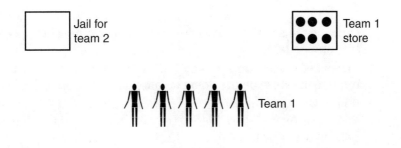

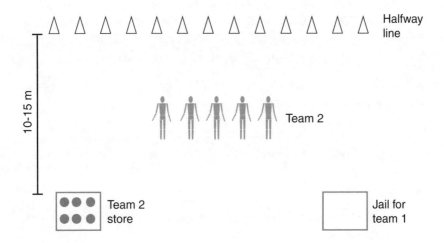

Figure 1.6

There are ten key rules which should help you explain the rules to the group, as follows.

1. When players enter the other team's half they can be tagged by their opponents.

2. Players tagged in the opposing team's area are 'sent to jail' in their opponent's half.

3. Players attack by running into the opposing team's half attempting to get into their store without being tagged. The store is a safe area where attackers cannot be tagged.

4. No defenders are allowed into their own store or into the jail in their own half.

5. Attackers are allowed to capture *one ball only* per attack.

6. When they can, attackers attempt to run back to their own half carrying the ball they have captured (again avoiding being tagged by opponents).

7. Attackers tagged on the way back must return the ball to the opponent's store before going to jail.

8. If attackers are successful in 'capturing a ball' this is placed in their own team's store before they attempt to get another one. Balls may not be passed.

9. Players in jail are allowed to come back into the game if a team-mate runs into the jail and tags them. In this instance both players must walk back to their own half before doing anything else in the game. This is a 'free walk back' as opponents cannot tag them.

10. The game continues for a set time (e.g., 5 minutes) or until one team has captured all of the other team's balls.

Safety Tips

▸ Warn participants to be careful of collisions.

▸ Ensure participants do not tag too hard.

ADVICE

- Ask questions to check understanding after explaining the rules.
- Watch for participants taking more than one ball at a time.
- This game is great to introduce strategy in game activities. Talking about teamwork, defending, attacking and game tactics can help to introduce the concept of strategy.

VARIATIONS

- **Sport-specific:** The game can be adapted to a variety of sports such as soccer, basketball and rugby. For example, in soccer or basketball, players have to dribble the ball back without being tagged. In rugby, introduce tackling when players are carrying a ball, depending on age or ability.

Catch and Release AGES 5-13

 EQUIPMENT

One bib per 6 to 10 participants, cones.

GAME

Cone out your working area. Choose some of the group to become chasers. Each chaser puts a bib on. There should be one chaser for every 6 to 10 participants. On beginning the game the chasers run around trying to tag the rest of the group.

When they are tagged, participants adopt and hold a particular position such as a balance. To be 'freed' from this held position, another participant has to crawl under or run around them. Continue for a set time (e.g., 45 to 60 seconds) or until all the participants have been tagged, then change the chasers.

Safety Tips

▶ Warn participants to be careful of collisions.

▶ Ensure chasers do not tag too hard.

ADVICE

- Only choose one chaser per 6 to 10 participants to keep the game going.
- The number of people chasing should also be relative to the size of the coned area.
- During the game, you can help free participants if you feel too many are static (i.e., in the caught position).

VARIATIONS

- **Game variation:** When instructing younger groups, try 'shower tag'. In this version, the participant's arm is held above their head to look like a shower when caught. To be released a free participant presses the shower on (by touching the caught participant's arm) and pretends to wash their face or body. Then both participants can run off.
- **Harder:** Play the game on all fours rather than running (but only on a suitable surface).

- **Harder:** Instead of 'tagging', the chasers could throw a sponge ball underarm and try to hit the others on the legs in order to catch them.
- **Sport-specific:** This game can be adapted to soccer. Chasers run round dribbling a ball and try to hit the runners below the knee with the ball to tag them.

Chasers  AGES 5-13

EQUIPMENT

One bib per 6 to 10 participants, cones.

GAME

Cone out your working area. Choose some of the group to become chasers. Chasers put the bibs on. There should be one chaser for every 6-10 participants. On beginning the game, the chasers run around trying to tag the rest of the group.

When they are tagged participants have to perform an activity as a challenge. This should be something fun, for example saying something funny or performing an animal impression. Alternatively it could be an activity such as five star jumps. Continue for a set time (e.g., 45 to 60 seconds), then change the chasers.

> **Safety Tips**
>
> ▸ Warn participants to be careful of collisions.
> ▸ Ensure chasers do not tag too hard.

ADVICE

- Only choose one chaser per 6 to 10 participants to keep the game going, depending on age and experience.
- The number of people chasing should also be relative to the size of the coned area.
- *Challenges should not be seen as a punishment. Make sure that no challenge is too strenuous or severe.*

VARIATIONS

- **Easier:** Play the game on all fours rather than running (but only on a suitable surface).
- **Game variation:** Instead of 'tagging', the chasers could throw a sponge ball underarm and try to hit the others on the legs in order to catch them.

Circle Hold AGES 5-13

EQUIPMENT

None.

GAME

Arrange the participants into pairs and number each person one or two. Those numbered one form an inner circle with an arm on the shoulder of the person standing next to them. Their partners should stand behind them to form an outer circle. Those in the outer circle should stand with their hands on their partner's shoulders (figure 1.7). On your command, all participants carry out your instructions as quickly as possible, always ensuring they maintain a grip on their partner. The following are some sample commands:

- Clockwise—participants run in a clockwise direction.
- Anti-clockwise—participants run in an anti-clockwise direction.
- Change—those in the outer circle switch places with the inner circle.
- One on—those in the outer circle release their grip and have to accelerate to catch the next person in the inner circle.
- One back—those in the outer circle release their grip and have to slow down then hold onto the next person back in the inner circle.

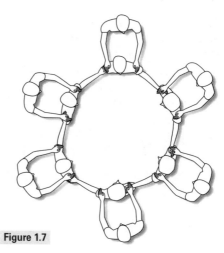

Figure 1.7

> ### Safety Tips
>
> ▸ Participants should not hold on to their partners'
>   shirts.
>
> ▸ Start at a slow speed until all the participants have an
>   understanding of the activity.

✹ ADVICE

- This game is good to use as a warm-up activity.
- Add one instruction at a time.
- Once participants have the basic idea, speed up the activity by changing the instructions more regularly.

✹ VARIATIONS

- **Easier/Harder:** Make up your own instructions to suit or challenge the group you are instructing.

Copy Command   AGES 5-10

✹ EQUIPMENT

Cones.

✹ GAME

This is a sporting variation of the game 'Simon says'. Cone out your working area. Participants jog or run round inside the coned area. Shout out instructions, which the participants only have to follow if the words 'instructor says . . .' are said before the instruction. Therefore, if you shouted 'instructor says sit on the floor', participants should sit on the floor. If you just said 'sit on the floor', they should carry on regardless.

> ### Safety Tips
>
> ▸ Warn participants to be careful of collisions.

ADVICE

The following are examples of commands:

- Hop on the right or left foot.
- Put a specific body part on the floor.
- Form a group of three.
- Run backwards.
- Skip sideways.

VARIATIONS

- **Game variation:** If your next activity involves the participants taking part in groups, finish the game by instructing participants to form groups of however many you want.
- **Sport-specific:** This activity can be adapted for a number of sports, such as soccer, by performing sport-specific skills or stopping the ball with a specific part of the body.

Do This, Do That
AGES **5-13**

EQUIPMENT

None.

GAME

This activity is good for use as part of a progressive warm-up. Participants find their own space in front of you so that they can all see your actions. Call out a number of actions, which the participants follow as if in an aerobics class.

You should warm up the participants by doing a variety of movements such as jumping on the spot or circling arms. As you move and the participants copy, the idea is to make the participants think and try to catch them out. Say 'do this' if you want the participants to replicate your movement. Say 'do that' if you don't want them to copy your movements. If the participants do copy you then they have to do a challenge of your choice.

ADVICE

- Move to new positions slowly to start with so that all the participants understand what is required.

VARIATIONS

- **Harder:** Participants work in their own little groups with one of them acting as the leader.

Freeze

AGES 5-13

EQUIPMENT

Cones.

GAME

Line the participants up between two cones and explain the rules of the game. Move to around 20 m away and stand with your back to them. Shout out a random number and count down from it, for example shout out the number five and count down '5-4-3-2-1'.

As soon as you start counting, the participants start running towards you trying to be the first to touch your back. On finishing the count down spin round quickly to face the group. You should have informed them to 'freeze' when you turn around, so the participants should be standing perfectly still. Anyone seen moving when you have turned should be sent back to the starting line. Repeat this until one person wins by being the first to touch your back.

ADVICE

- When playing the game with children under six, be selective of whom you send back to the start first to avoid tears.

- Watch for participants moving before you start counting when you have your back turned.

 ## VARIATIONS

- **Sport-specific:** This can be adapted for games involving dribbling such as basketball and soccer. The winner would be the first person to pass their ball through your legs.

Group Of AGES **5-16**

 ## EQUIPMENT

Cones.

 ## GAME

Cone out your working area. Participants run around the area in different directions, slowly building up speed. Shout out a number (e.g., 'five'). The participants then have to find a group of five and sit down as soon as possible. Hurry the participants by counting down the seconds they have left then shouting '3-2-1 stop!' Any participants who can't find a group perform a fun challenge before the next round. When each new round starts participants must run around on their own constantly changing direction, thus helping to avoid forming groups of the same participants each time.

> ### Safety Tips
>
> ▶ Warn participants to be careful of collisions.

ADVICE

- Be strict on timing. Any participants not in a group when you shout 'stop' must perform the fun challenge.

VARIATIONS

- **Game variation:** Participants are given a point each time they get into a group in the specified time. Play for a set period of time and the player with the most points at the end wins the game.

Hills and Hollows AGES **5-13**

EQUIPMENT

Three cones per participant.

GAME

Separate participants into two teams and position them on opposite sides of the working area about 20 m apart. Scatter the cones in between them with half the cones standing the right way up as hills (figure 1.8) and half upside down as hollows (figure 1.9). One team works to turn the hills into hollows while the other team competes against them, turning the hollows into hills. After 45 to 60 seconds stop the game and count up the hills and the hollows to see which team has turned over the most cones.

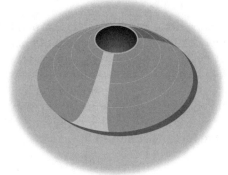

Figure 1.8

Figure 1.9

ADVICE

- Encourage fair play so that participants do not turn cones after you have stopped the game.
- Also inform the participants that if anyone is seen to continue after the stop command, the opposing team will be awarded bonus points.
- Do not allow cones to be guarded. Players must move to another cone as soon as they have turned one over.

VARIATIONS

- **Game variation:** Use a relay system where one or more players run out and can change a number of cones before returning to the line. The other player(s) then take their turn to run out.
- **Harder:** The game can be played on hands and feet.
- **Harder:** Participants can only use their feet to turn over the cones.

Hit but Not Out   AGES 5-16

EQUIPMENT

Benches, four large sponge balls, one bib between two.

GAME

Split the sport hall into four sections using benches put across the width of the hall. Separate the group into two teams. One team stands in one of the middle sections, while the opposing team stands in the other one (figure 1.10). Each team has two sponge balls, which participants throw at opponents, trying to hit them below the waist. Opponents try to avoid being hit by dodging out of the way.

If any participant is hit below the waist, they move to the 'hit area' behind the other team's section. These players can throw any balls that land in that area back at their opponents. When all the participants on one team are in their opponents' hit area the opposing team wins.

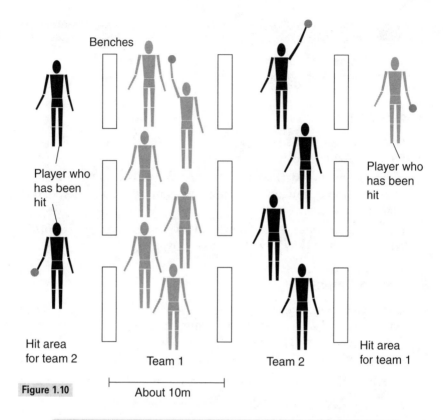

Benches

Player who
has been
hit

Player who
has been
hit

Hit area
for team 2

Team 1

Team 2

Hit area
for team 1

Figure 1.10

About 10m

Safety Tips

▶ Use low throws only to avoid people getting hit in the face.

▶ Ensure participants do not throw the ball too hard.

▶ Use soft balls only.

▶ Don't allow players to stand on benches.

ADVICE

- This activity is ideally played in a small sport hall.
- Participants in the hit area can only use a ball when it goes into that area—no reaching over.
- Put in more balls to speed up the game.

VARIATIONS

- **Easier/Harder:** Use wider or narrower middle areas to increase or decrease the difficulty.

- **Game variation:** Players in the hit area can move back to the middle section if they hit an opponent. This keeps the game going for longer.

Hoop Defender   AGES 8-16

EQUIPMENT

One to four large sponge balls, 10 to 16 hoops, one bib between two.

GAME

This game is best played in a sport hall or gym. Set up the area as shown in figure 1.11. Ideally a basketball or netball court should be used. Two teams stand at opposite ends of the court inside a semi-circle (i.e., the three-point line on a basketball court or the shooting area on a netball court). Place half the hoops in front of one team's area and the other half in front of the opposing team's area. If you do not have hoops use cones or chalk to mark out metre-wide areas around each team.

Participants run to the opposite end and throw sponge balls at opponents, trying to hit them below the waist. The thrower is not allowed to enter the area beyond the hoops to throw at their opponents. After throwing, participants must return to their side.

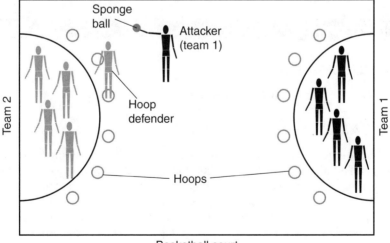

Figure 1.11

If an opponent is hit they have to stand inside a hoop in front of their team-mates. These 'hoop defenders' can block any balls thrown at the rest of their team. If they catch a ball they are back in the game. If all the participants in the semi-circle are hit, then the opposing team wins the game. Time the game, and if it has not been completed, stop after 3 to 5 minutes. The winning team will be the one with the fewest players standing in the hoops.

Safety Tips

▶ Allow low throws only to avoid people getting hit in the face.

▶ Use soft balls only.

● ADVICE

• Put in more balls to speed up the game.

• Start with two sponge balls and add more as the participants become familiar with the game.

● VARIATIONS

• **Game variation:** Players are allowed to hit opponents who are running through the middle area if they are in possession of a ball.

Jailbreak   AGES 5-13

● EQUIPMENT

One bib per 6 to 10 participants, cones.

● GAME

Cone out a boundary for the game. In the centre use some more cones to mark out a 'jail'. This should be a square around 7 × 7 m. Choose some of the group to become chasers. Each of them puts a bib on. There should be one chaser for every six to eight participants. Chasers start by running around trying to tag the rest of the group. Once participants have been tagged they must stand inside the jail. Other participants who have not been tagged must try to free the captured ones by running into the jail and tagging the prisoners. The chasers are not allowed to go inside the jail at any time. Every so often change the chasers.

Safety Tips

▶ Warn participants to be careful of collisions.

▶ Ensure chasers do not tag too hard.

ADVICE

- The chasers must seek a balance between chasing and guarding the jail.
- It is important that you choose a suitable number of chasers for the game to last.

VARIATIONS

- **Game variation:** This game can be played in teams, using timed innings.
- **Harder:** Vary the positions prisoners adopt while in jail and vary freeing methods. For example prisoners could curl into a ball in the prison and in order to be freed another participant has to step over and tag them on the back.

Linda's Game

AGES **5-13**

EQUIPMENT

One beanbag or any type of sport ball each.

GAME

Put the participants into equal teams of between four and six. The whole group should then stand in a large circle, but teams should stand together. There should be a gap between each team, and each participant should be numbered (see figure 1.12). Participants sit down facing the centre of the circle. Place some beanbags (or balls) in the centre of the circle, making sure there is one fewer than the number of teams you have, for example four beanbags for five teams.

Shout out a number like 'three'. The participant numbered three from each team stands up and runs clockwise around the outside of the circle. Once they have completed a lap, participants run through the gap they were sitting in and attempt to pick up a beanbag. Those who pick up a beanbag score a point for their team. Place the beanbags back on the

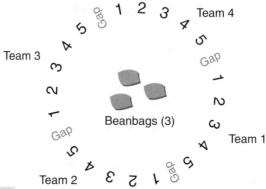

Figure 1.12

floor and when the participants are back sitting in their place, call out another number. Continue until one team has reached a set number of points (e.g., 15) or for a set time (e.g., 5 minutes).

> ### Safety Tips
>
> ▶ Ensure the beanbags are spaced out in the middle of the circle to prevent participants from clashing heads during the race for a beanbag.
>
> ▶ Only play on a non-slippery surface.
>
> ▶ When participants are not running, they should be sitting cross-legged and should not obstruct the other runners.

● ADVICE

- With younger participants, use coloured bibs so that they can see where the rest of their team-mates are sitting.
- Change participants' numbers within their team so that they have a chance to race against different opponents.

● VARIATIONS

- **Game variation:** Shout two numbers at a time, but increase the number of beanbags in the middle area.
- **Harder:** Decrease the number of beanbags.
- **Harder:** Have two coloured beanbags in the centre area and assign a different value to the beanbags.

Line Tag AGES **5-13**

 ## EQUIPMENT

Floor with markings on (e.g., tennis courts or a sport hall floor), one bib per four to six participants.

GAME

This game is best played inside a sport hall that has a variety of courts marked out. The lines are likely to be of different colours and will intersect each other. Choose some of the group to become chasers, who each put a bib on. There should be one chaser for every four to six participants. Chasers start by running around trying to tag the rest of the group. All participants must stay on the lines and are not allowed to jump from one line to another. Chasers must be on the same line as the person they are pursuing to tag them. All participants can change direction and start following a different-coloured line, but only where the lines intersect. Tagged participants must perform a fun challenge before rejoining the game. Count how many times participants are tagged by the chasers in a set time period (e.g., 45 to 60 seconds). Change the chasers and begin again.

Safety Tips

▶ Warn participants to be careful of collisions.

▶ Ensure chasers do not tag too hard.

ADVICE

- It is important that you choose a suitable number of chasers for the game to last.
- Participants can overtake others but must return to the line straight away.
- Chasers will find it easier if they work together to try to trap the participants they are pursuing.

VARIATIONS

- **Game variation:** Allow participants to move on only one colour of line.
- **Game variation:** This game can be played in teams, for example with a group of 16 participants split into four teams (4 in each).

Each team takes a turn to be the chasers and has 60 seconds to tag as many people as possible. Count up the number tagged by each team, with the team scoring the most winning the game.

- **Game variation:** Allow the participants to step from line to line providing they are within an easy reaching distance. They must not touch the floor where there is no line.

Mass Invasion AGES 8-16

EQUIPMENT

Cones, six hoops, 10 beanbags (five of one colour and five of another), four coloured balls (again two of each colour is preferable), two sets of different-coloured sashes or bibs (rugby 'tag belts' can also be used). There should be around three sashes or bibs for each participant (e.g., for 12 participants there may be 18 blue sashes and 18 red sashes).

GAME

This activity is an invasion game that you need to explain carefully, but it is one your group should really enjoy playing. You will need plenty of space—an area the size of a soccer pitch is advisable. Participants are separated into two teams, with each team named after the colour of their sashes (e.g., a 'blue' team wearing blue sashes and a 'red' team wearing red sashes.) Participants should tuck one sash into the top of their shorts at their side or back. This should be clearly visible and not hidden under their tee-shirt or pullover.

The hoops are set up as shown in figure 1.13 with each team having three hoops at their end of the field. One hoop keeps the spare sashes, another is called the 'trophy cabinet' and the final one is named the 'storage area'. Cone out an area around the storage areas about 10 m in diameter. Participants defending their own storage area are not allowed to enter this coned area. Place the coloured balls and beanbags in the appropriate team's storage area.

When the game begins, participants try to 'steal' items from their opponents. They can take a sash from an opponent or try to get a ball or beanbag from the storage areas. They must not take anything from the hoop containing the spare sashes or the opposing team's trophy cabinet. Participants can defend their team's storage area by stealing sashes from the opposing team's attackers. Any items taken from an opponent should be placed in the trophy cabinet. Participants must only be in possession of *one stolen item* at any time during the game. Any player in possession

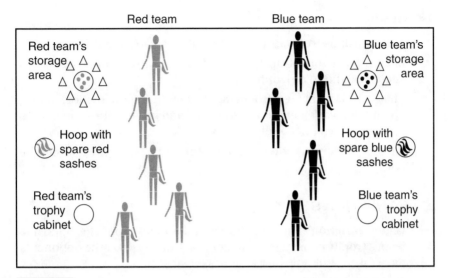

Figure 1.13

of a stolen item is out of the game. This means they cannot take a sash from an opponent but cannot have their own sash taken either. As soon as they have placed the item in their team's trophy cabinet they can join in the fun again. Any player who has had their own sash taken is also out until they go to the hoops where the spare sashes are kept and place one into their shorts.

The following points are awarded for taking items at the end of the game.

- One point is awarded for each sash taken.
- Five points are awarded for each beanbag taken.
- Ten points are awarded for each ball taken.

The game should continue for a set time (e.g., 7 to 10 minutes). At the end of this time count up the amount of points scored.

Safety Tips

▶ This can be a very tiring game, so remember to give rest periods between games.

▶ Warn participants to be careful of collisions.

▶ Participants cannot grab opponents' clothing to slow them down while taking a sash.

ADVICE

- Ask questions to check understanding after explaining the rules.
- Ensure participants do not take items from the opposing team's spare sash hoop or trophy cabinet.
- This game is great for introducing strategy in game activities. Talking about teamwork, defending, attacking and game tactics can help to introduce the concept of strategy.
- Ensure participants do not join in the game when they should be out.

VARIATIONS

- **Game variation:** Participants can take items from the opposing team's trophy cabinet (i.e., stealing back objects that the opponents have taken) but not their spare sashes hoop.
- **Game variation:** Participants can take items from any hoop.
- **Game variation:** There is no 'out' rule for participants in possession of a stolen item. If an opponent takes their sash then they must give the stolen item to this person. The sash should be placed in the trophy cabinet, but the stolen item should be put back in the store.

 AGES **5-10**

EQUIPMENT

Cones.

GAME

This activity involves thinking and understanding and is good for use as part of a progressive warm-up. Cone out your working area. Participants move around the area. When you shout out a command, they must do the opposite. For example, if you shout 'right hand' then participants have to touch the floor with their left hand, and vice versa.

> **Safety Tips**
>
> ▶ Warn participants to be careful of collisions.
> ▶ Remember to start slowly and increase the intensity towards the end if using as part of a warm-up.

ADVICE

- Use only two or three of the sets of commands at the beginning, as the participants will forget the commands if you give them all at the same time. Add the new commands one set at a time. The following are some examples of sets of commands:
    - Right hand—touch left hand on floor/Left hand—touch right hand on floor.
    - Jump—sit down then stand back up/Sit—jump in the air.
    - Run—walk round the area/Walk—run round the area.
    - Forward—move backwards around the area/Backward—move forwards round the area.
    - Hop right—hop on left foot/Hop left—hop on right foot.
    - Sideskip right—sideskip to the left/Sideskip left—sideskip to the right.

VARIATIONS

- **Game variation:** Change to doing the actions correctly. For example, Right hand—touch right hand on floor/Left hand—touch left hand on floor. Alternate between correct actions and opposites every 10 to 15 seconds to confuse participants.

Partner Run AGES 5-16

EQUIPMENT

Cones.

GAME

This is a good activity for use as part of a progressive warm-up. Participants should work with a partner, facing each other about 20 m apart. Use cones to mark each participant's starting position. Participants should number themselves one and two, form two parallel lines and listen for their number to be called. When you have called their number participants should jog towards their partner, go around them and return to their original start position. Instead of just jogging, change the action they carry out each time their number is called.

The following are some examples:

- Sidestepping
- Heel flicking (flicking heels off backside while running)
- Crawling on all fours
- Jogging to their partner, crawling through their legs then jogging back
- Hopping on right foot to partner, running round them twice then hopping back on the opposite foot

Safety Tips

▸ Ensure participants are standing around 3 to 5 m from the person next to them so that when their partner moves around them they do not collide with others.

▸ Ensure participants do not grab or spin their partner as they move around them.

ADVICE

- If used as part of a warm-up ensure movements are progressive. Begin with less intense movements such as jogging and include more vigorous ones towards the end of the warm-up.
- Use your imagination when designing movements for the participants. Make them fun and appropriate to the age of the participants. With younger participants, animal actions or funny walks work well and you can also ask them for their own ideas.

VARIATIONS

- **Harder:** The activity can be changed to become a race when a participant's number is called out.
- **Sport-specific:** It can be adapted for use in a variety of different sports by carrying out relevant skills when travelling to and from partners. For basketball, dribble forwards to partner, round them then dribble facing backwards as they return to their start position.

Put Out, Pick Up Relay

● EQUIPMENT

Cones, one beanbag between two (or any suitable object that can be carried and placed out by the participants), hoops.

● GAME

This is a variation of a relay that is usually carried out as a competitive team race. Set up the cones and hoops as shown in figure 1.14. Arrange the participants in teams of four to eight. Each team forms a line with the first in line facing the hoop they are going to run to (see figure 1.14 for set-up). On the floor beside the first person in each team should be their beanbags. There should be half as many beanbags as there are members in their team. For example, if there are eight participants in the team, there should be four beanbags.

The first person runs out with a beanbag, puts it into the hoop and returns to the start. As soon as they return the next person replicates this process. This continues until all the beanbags have been put out. The next person in each team to go must retrieve *one beanbag* and return

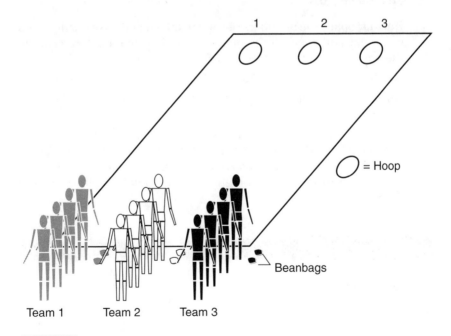

Figure 1.14

this to the start. The activity ends when all the beanbags have been retrieved. In each team the first half of the line put out a beanbag while the second half of the group pick up a beanbag. The team completing this first wins the relay. The activity can be repeated in a number of ways using more hoops or different amounts of beanbags (see Variations for some of these).

> ### Safety Tips
>
> ▶ Ensure you have completed a thorough warm-up before carrying out this activity as it is very intense.

ADVICE

- If there is not an equal number in each team, some participants run twice to equalise the amount of runs. Regularly change those running twice to avoid players getting too tired.
- Try to pick teams with a mixture of abilities to ensure all the participants are motivated.

VARIATIONS

- **Harder:** Space the members of each team out and have participants go 'under and over' all the members of their team before running the sprint.
- **Harder:** Change to weaving in and out of the team before running.
- **Harder:** Have more than one hoop in a line. Participants put out a beanbag in each.
- **Harder:** Participants who are putting out a beanbag run out to a 'throwing line', then have to throw it into the hoop before running back. If they miss they can have two further attempts to get it into the hoop (throwing from the line each time) before they return to the start.

Roller Ball AGES **5-16**

EQUIPMENT

One ball of any type between two, cones.

GAME

This is an activity that can be used as part of a progressive warm-up or to practise relevant sport skills. Cone out your working area. Arrange participants in pairs with a ball between them. One participant rolls the ball in front of his or her partner for them to run on to and pick up. The partner should do the same, rolling the ball in a different direction. With all the groups working in the same area, participants need to work out which space to roll the ball into and time the roll so that the ball does not touch anyone else or hit any other balls. This means they will have to make decisions about where and when to roll the ball. The activity involves and develops timing and targeting abilities to ensure balls do not collide, in addition to the skills needed to pick the ball up.

Safety Tips

▶ Warn participants to be careful of collisions.

▶ If playing indoors, still cone out a boundary. This should be at least 2 m from the wall and should help to avoid participants running into the walls.

ADVICE

- Make sure participants are working cooperatively and not rolling the ball too hard.
- Make sure there is plenty of room for beginners and younger participants.

VARIATIONS

- **Harder:** Make the area smaller to make the practice more difficult.
- **Harder:** Only use the non-dominant hand to roll and pick up the ball.
- **Harder:** Instruct the participant picking up the ball to do a dodge so that the 'roller' needs to roll after the dodge and in the direction of the second run.
- **Large groups:** Participants can work in groups of three or four.
- **Sport-specific:** This game can be adapted to specific sports such as soccer, basketball or hockey by passing the ball instead of rolling it.

Shuttles

● EQUIPMENT

Possibly cones.

● GAME

This is an activity that can be used as part of a warm-up or as races where participants work against the rest of the group. Cone out your working area. Arrange the cones in lines so that there is a starting line and four other lines about 5 to 8 m apart (see figure 1.15). Line the participants up on the starting line and call out the number of the line(s) that the participants must run to. Therefore, if you shout numbers one and four, then the participants run out to line one, return to the start, then run to line four before returning to the start.

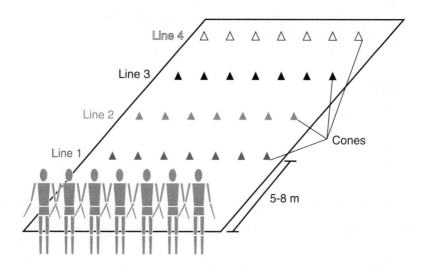

Figure 1.15

Safety Tips

► Ensure participants are thoroughly warmed up if participants are sprinting through the shuttles.

► Ensure adequate rest periods between each turn.

ADVICE

The following are examples of some of the commands:

- Hop out on right foot and back on left foot.
- Run backwards.
- Move on hands and feet.
- Skip sideways.
- Bunny hop.

VARIATIONS

- **Easier:** Participants can get a longer rest between sprints if you group them.
- **Harder:** Make it a race to add competition.
- **Sport-specific:** The game can be adapted to specific sports by using relevant skills when travelling between lines. For example, soccer could be used by dribbling to the line with the right foot and back with the left foot.

Stars and Stripes  AGES 5-13

EQUIPMENT

Cones (to mark out lines for participants to run towards).

GAME

Arrange participants into pairs and instruct them to stand opposite their partners about 2 m apart (see figure 1.16). Name all the participants in one of the lines 'stars' and name all the participants in the other line 'stripes'. Two lines of cones are placed on the ground, one on either side of the participants. Shout 'stars' and all the stars quickly turn and run towards the nearest line of cones. In this instance the stripes must chase after their partner, trying to tag them before they get to the line of cones.

If the star reaches the line before being tagged they gain a point. However, if the stripe tags their partner before they get to the line then they gain the point. If you call out 'stripe' then the opposite occurs with the stripe running for the nearest line and their partner trying to tag them before they get there. After each race participants should return to their starting positions ready for you to call out the next star or stripe. Participants should play the best out of five or seven and should keep score of their points.

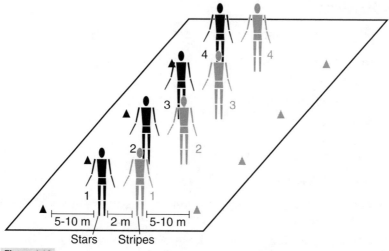

Figure 1.16

Safety Tips

▸ Warn participants to be careful of collisions.

▸ Ensure chasers do not tag too hard.

▸ Participants should turn and run in a straight line towards the cones and not cut across other participants' paths.

ADVICE

- Linger on the 'st' part of the call and occasionally call out words such as 'st . . . rawberries' to keep the participants guessing.
- Change partners regularly.
- Ensure participants are correctly warmed up before this activity.

VARIATIONS

- **Easier/Harder:** Vary the starting positions of the participants. For example, they may sit or lie opposite their partners.
- **Game variation:** Change the names used, to 'crumbs and crusts', for example.
- **Sport-specific:** This suits various games such as soccer or hockey that involve dribbling. In this case participants all have a ball beside them. When their name is called they have to dribble their ball to the line before being tagged. The chaser does not dribble a ball.

Sticky Toffee AGES **5-13**

 EQUIPMENT

Two bibs, cones.

 GAME

Cone out your working area. Choose two chasers, who put bibs on. The chasers start by running around trying to tag other participants. When a chaser tags another participant, this person becomes a chaser with the two of them joining hands. Holding hands, the two of them continue trying to tag others.

The next person tagged joins them to make a three. If a group of three chasers manages to tag another participant, instead of making a line of four chasers they separate into two pairs. The game continues until all participants have been tagged. Start a new game with the participants who were tagged last from the previous game becoming the chasers.

Safety Tips

▶ Warn participants to be careful of collisions.

▶ Ensure chasers do not tag too hard.

▶ Encourage chasers to hold on tightly and work together to tag others.

 ADVICE

- Instruct chasers that they can only tag other participants if they are still linked.
- It is a good game to play if you want to do pair work at the end of the game as participants have a partner.
- When chasing, participants need communication skills to work as a team.
- Make the area smaller or bigger depending on how quickly the chasers tag the others (a bigger area should make the game last longer).

 VARIATIONS

- **Small groups:** When you are coaching smaller groups, it is possible to keep the line building up when participants are tagged, making a long line of chasers. This can work with fewer than eight in a group.

- **Sport-specific:** This can be adapted to games that involve dribbling such as soccer and basketball. With basketball, all the participants have a ball except the chasers. The participants with a ball dribble it continuously in the area while the chasers try to knock the balls out. Participants who lose their balls make sure the ball does not roll back into the area before joining hands with the chaser.

Tails

EQUIPMENT

One bib or sash per participant, cones.

GAME

Cone out your working area. Choose one or two participants to be chasers. Chasers put the bibs on. The rest of the participants should tuck a bib into the back of their shorts as a tail. This should be clearly visible and not hidden under their tee-shirt or pullover. Chasers start by running around trying to pull tails off the other participants. Those who lose their tails become chasers and help to get the remaining tails. Continue for a set time (e.g., 45 to 60 seconds) or until there is only one participant left with a tail in. Change the chasers and begin again.

> **Safety Tips**
>
> ▶ This can be a very tiring game, so remember to give rest periods between games.
>
> ▶ Warn participants to be careful of collisions.
>
> ▶ Participants may not grab opponents' clothing to slow them down while taking a tail.

ADVICE

- Once the chasers have taken a tail they should hand it to you before continuing with the game.
- Ensure all participants stay inside the working area.

● *VARIATIONS*

- **Easier:** Participants with tails start at one end of the working area and run to the other side without being caught. Chasers have to pull the tails out as the other participants run past them.
- **Game variation:** Choose a number of chasers, but when they grab a tail the two change roles (i.e., this chaser puts the tail in while the other participant becomes a chaser).
- **Game variation:** The game can be adapted into a team game by using two different-coloured sets of bibs. Participants try to take a bib from an opponent. If they manage to do this they give the bib to the instructor and gain a point for their team. The instructor then gives the bib back to the person it was taken from but keeps score of how many points are scored by each team. The team scoring the most at the end of a set time wins the game.

Team Drop
AGES **11-16**

● *EQUIPMENT*

One volleyball or other similar type of sport ball per 8 to 12 participants, cones.

● *GAME*

This is an activity that is well suited for use in a volleyball session. Arrange the participants into groups of 8 to 12, then separate each group into two equal teams. Number the teams 1 and 2. Cone out the playing area. This should be a small square surrounded by a larger square (see figure 1.17). Team 1 stands inside the small square, while team 2 stands outside it (but still inside the large square). A member of team 2 takes the ball and serves it. The server stands at the edge of the large square and throws the ball underhand into the smaller square for the opposing team to deal. The ball must pass above head height when travelling towards team 1. After releasing the ball, the server is allowed to come back into the large square. Team 1 has to keep the ball off the floor using arms and hands. After taking three touches players should attempt to hit the ball so that it lands on the floor in team 2's area.

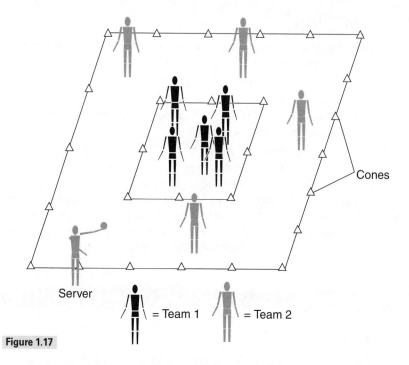

Cones

Server

= Team 1   = Team 2

Figure 1.17

If team 1 is unsuccessful in playing the correct number of touches or the ball does not land on the floor in the correct area, team 2 is awarded a point. Then the server takes another turn. If team 1 is successful in taking the required number of touches and playing the ball onto the floor, then service is won. In this instance the teams will swap positions and team 1 will now have service. Team 2 can defend by playing the ball back into the smaller square, again trying to do this without the ball touching the floor. When defending the outside area participants are only allowed one touch to play the ball. Play for a set time (e.g., 5 minutes) or until one team scores a set number of points (e.g., 11 points) to decide who wins.

Safety Tips

▶ Warn participants to be careful of collisions.

▶ Ensure the ball the participants are playing with is suitable for the activity. Ideally use a volleyball.

▶ Participants must not hit the ball hard towards the ground. Insist that all shots into the opposing team's area must travel above head height before landing on the ground.

ADVICE

- Demonstrate how points are scored to ensure all participants understand. The points system is the same as in badminton where participants can only score points when they have the service.
- Participants should look for gaps in the opposing team's area when playing the ball into their area.
- Ensure the size of the areas suits the ability of the performers. Larger areas increase the difficulty.

VARIATIONS

- **Easier:** With younger children the game can be played using a balloon instead of a ball.
- **Easier/Harder:** Change the difficulty level by changing the number of touches each team must have.
- **Sport-specific:** The game can be adapted to soccer, but participants cannot use their hands to keep the ball off the floor.

Team Take   AGES 5-13

EQUIPMENT

Cones, four hoops, one sport ball of any type each (cones, beanbags, shuttles or other similar objects could be used as an alternative).

GAME

This is a relay activity with a twist. Cone out a square working area. Place all the balls on the floor in the centre of this area. Arrange the participants into four teams of three to five. Teams line up in each corner just outside the area, with the hoop placed on the floor in front of them (see figure 1.18). The first person in each team starts by running to the centre of the area and picking up a ball, running back, placing the ball in their hoop, then tagging the next team-mate in the line before joining the back of the queue. Each team repeats this sequence until all the balls have been taken from the centre of the area. Count up the amount of balls taken by each team to decide who wins that round, then return the balls to the centre for the next one.

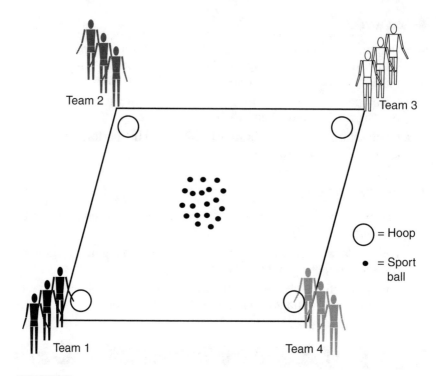

Team 2

Team 3

◯ = Hoop

● = Sport ball

Team 1

Team 4

Figure 1.18

Safety Tips

▸ Ensure the balls are spread out slightly in the centre to avoid collisions.

▸ Warn participants to be careful of collisions.

ADVICE

- Ensure participants take one ball at a time.
- If possible use more balls than there are participants to ensure the activity lasts for a suitable length of time.
- Try to have an odd number of balls, as this ensures all groups do not finish with the same number of points.
- After each round ask participants to bring the balls back to the centre, not throw them.
- When playing variations of this activity ensure that there is no 'guarding' of collected balls.

VARIATIONS

- **Game variation:** Inform participants that after all the balls have been collected from the centre, they may go and take a ball from an opponent's hoop.

- **Game variation:** Allow all participants to run at the same time. Again insist that all the balls in the centre are collected before they can start taking balls from opponent's hoops.

- **Harder:** Participants are only allowed to retrieve the ball with a specific part of their body (e.g., between the knees).

- **Sport-specific:** This game can be adapted to become a dribbling game for sports such as basketball, hockey and soccer.

Thawed Out   AGES **5-13**

 EQUIPMENT

Cones.

GAME

This is another tag game variation. Cone out your working area. Set up a game of tag, choosing some of the group to become chasers. Each of them puts a bib on. There should be one chaser for every 8 to 10 runners. The chasers are called 'Mr/Mrs Freeze'. Choose one runner to be your 'Mr/Mrs Heat', but do not let the chasers know whom you have chosen. Mr or Mrs Freeze starts by running around trying to tag the rest of the group. If a participant is tagged they stand still and pretend to be frozen. They are allowed back into the game if they are touched by Mr or Mrs Heat (i.e., they have been 'thawed out'). If Mr or Mrs Heat have been tagged then the chasers should be able to tag all the rest without them being able to move. Play until all participants have been tagged or for a set time (e.g., 1 to 2 minutes), whichever is sooner.

> ### Safety Tips
>
> ▶ Warn participants to be careful of collisions.
> ▶ Ensure chasers do not tag too hard.

✸ ADVICE

- Make sure you explain the game well and demonstrate so that the activity runs smoothly.
- You can add tactics to the game by telling all those 'unfrozen' to tag those who are frozen to confuse the chasers. Those who have been thawed out can also confuse the chasers by delaying their movements after they have been tagged by Mr or Mrs Heat.

✸ VARIATIONS

- **Easier/Harder:** Change the difficulty by altering the number of chasers.
- **Sport-specific:** The game can be adapted to soccer by dribbling a ball around the area. The chasers try to hit other participants' soccer balls with their own to 'freeze' them.

Total Relay   AGES 5-13

✸ EQUIPMENT

Cones.

✸ GAME

Use this activity as part of a progressive warm-up. It is a variation of a normal relay. Arrange the group into teams of four to five. For each team use a cone for the starting point and then place a cone on the floor up to 20 m away for the participants to run to. Each team lines up behind the start (see figure 1.19). In a normal relay, when the relay starts the first participant in each team runs out to a specified point and then runs back. On completion, players tag the next in their team, who repeats this process and then joins the back of their team's line. The relay ends when all of the team have taken their turn and the line is back in its starting order.

The difference with this activity is that instead of standing still waiting for their turn, participants have to do an exercise while they wait. All the participants complete the same activity while waiting for their turn to run. Examples of activities could be star jumps, sit-ups, squat thrusts or a range of other exercises. If used as part of a warm-up, continue for a set time (e.g., 3 to 5 minutes), but change the exercise those in the line have to do every 15 to 20 seconds.

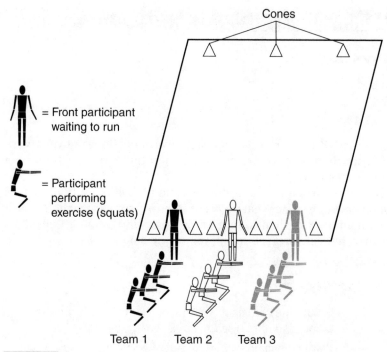

Figure 1.19

ADVICE

- Make sure the participants have enough space to do the activity while waiting in line.
- Ensure there is enough space between groups to avoid collisions.
- Warn participants to be careful of collisions.

VARIATIONS

- **Game variation:** As one participant is running, the person who is now at the front chooses an activity while waiting for their turn to run. The rest of the line copies this activity.
- **Harder:** Make the relay into a race.
- **Harder:** Instead of all those in line doing the same exercise, choose a different exercise for each position.
- **Sport-specific:** The relay can be modified for use in most sports. An example could be in basketball, where participants dribble the ball instead of just running. Those waiting for their turn perform a skill, such as circling the ball round their waist, while they are waiting.

Touch and Go! AGES 5-10

 EQUIPMENT

Cones.

 GAME

Use this activity as part of a progressive warm-up. Cone out your working area. Participants move around the area in different directions, slowly building up speed.

Once the participants are moving around, call out a body part. The participants must place that body part on the floor as quickly as possible, get straight back up then continue moving around the area. Call out parts like nose, left ear, knees, bottom, tummy or hands.

> ### Safety Tips
>
> ▶ Ensure the participants have sufficient space in which to move to minimise the risk of collisions.
>
> ▶ Warn participants to be careful of collisions.
>
> ▶ Participants should touch the floor gently with the specified body part.

 ADVICE

- Encourage the participants to keep them enthused about the game.

 VARIATIONS

- **Sport-specific:** This game can be adapted to soccer. Participants dribble their ball round the area. When a body part is called out, participants must touch their ball with the body part before continuing.

Trio Dodge

 EQUIPMENT

None.

 GAME

Arrange the participants into groups of four. Choose one chaser from each group. The rest join hands to form a ring. Of these three, nominate one to be chased. The chaser starts by trying to tag the nominee on the back. The three participants in the ring dodge around to avoid the chaser. If the chaser manages to tag the nominee then choose a new chaser and start the game again.

Safety Tips

▶ The participants in the ring must work together to avoid colliding or tripping over each other.

▶ Ensure participants in the ring hold hands tightly to avoid letting go and spinning out of control.

ADVICE

- The participants in the ring have to rotate the shape quickly to react to the movement of the chaser.
- The chaser cannot cut through the middle of the ring to tag the nominee.
- If the chaser cannot tag the nominee in 45 to 60 seconds, change the chaser and start the activity again.

VARIATIONS

- **Harder:** The chaser has to catch all of the players in the ring in a specified order before changing roles.
- **Harder:** Instead of three participants forming a ring, play with four or five participants.

Basketball
and
Netball Games

The activities in this chapter relate to basketball and netball. The activities

- include a mixture of games, warm-up activities and skill practices, and
- can be used to develop passing, dribbling and shooting skills.

You can adapt the passing and shooting activities for netball sessions. In most cases the rules for netball will be similar, but you may need to make a few modifications. To find out whether the activity is suitable for netball consult the Variations section of each activity.

Most activities can be played by children of all ages, but try to ensure that basketballs and basket sizes are relevant to their age and ability. As a basic guide

- under-eights play with a size 5 basketball,
- under-twelves play with a size 6 basketball,
- over-twelves play with a full-size basketball (size 7).

The most important thing is that all participants experience success. You should use your own judgement when deciding what equipment to use.

Follow the Leader   AGES **5-16**

● EQUIPMENT

One basketball each.

● GAME

Use this activity as part of a progressive warm-up. Arrange the participants into small groups of two to five. Each group should stand in a line and every participant should have a basketball. The first participant moves around the area performing a skill with his or her basketball. The rest of the group copy the actions of the leader. After a specified time the leader drops to the back of the line. The next participant takes over choosing their own skill, while the rest of the group copies his or her actions.

> **Safety Tips**
>
> ▶ Advise participants to stay at least 1 m behind the person in front.
> ▶ Do not allow groups to weave in and out of each other, to avoid collisions.

● ADVICE

- Ensure the size of the basketballs is appropriate for the age and experience of participants.
- Change the leader every 20 to 40 seconds.

- Provide some examples to give the groups ideas:
    - Dribbling with the right or left hand
    - Circling the basketball around the waist
    - Dribbling high or low
    - Bouncing the basketball while sitting on the floor

VARIATIONS

- **Game variation:** You can lead the line.
- **Game variation:** Allow use of the baskets for shooting and lay-up skills.
- **Netball:** Play with the same rules as basketball.
- **Small groups:** Have one line instead of lots of smaller ones.
- **Sport-specific:** Modify for a number of different sports (e.g., soccer, hockey and rugby) by performing sport-specific skills.

Hit It

AGES **5-13**

EQUIPMENT

One basketball and large cone per two participants.

GAME

This activity develops passing skills. Arrange the participants into pairs, giving each pair a basketball and a cone. Participants stand around 15 m apart with the cone in the centre of the space between them (see figure 2.1). Participants take turns trying to hit the cone by throwing the basketball at it. Between each participant and the basketball is the opponent's 'winning line'. The game continues until one player has knocked the cone towards their opponent and over the winning line.

> ### Safety Tips
>
> ▶ Ensure participants are throwing accurately and not too hard.

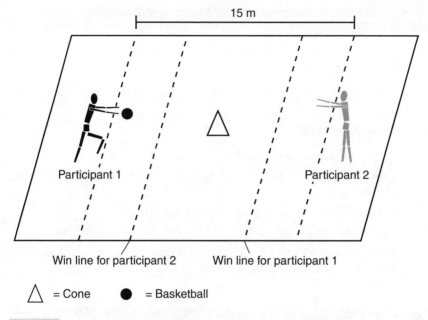

Figure 2.1

☀ ADVICE

- Ensure the size of the basketballs is appropriate for participants' age and experience.
- The target can be a large cone, a soft basketball or an alternative. Ideally the target should take three or four hits to be moved across the winning line. The target should be durable to withstand being hit repeatedly by a basketball.

☀ VARIATIONS

- **Game variation:** The game can be played in teams (e.g., four participants per team trying to hit one to three cones over the winning line).
- **Netball:** Play with the same rules as basketball.
- **Sport-specific:** The game can be adapted to other sports that involve passing skills. Kicking the ball at the target in soccer is one example.

Knockout AGES **5-16**

EQUIPMENT

One basketball each, one bib per four to eight participants, cones.

GAME

This activity develops dribbling skills. Cone out your working area and choose some of the group to become chasers. Each of them puts a bib on. There should be one chaser for every four to eight participants. All the participants stand inside the working area with a basketball, except for the chasers who stand at the side without one.

When the game begins those in the area try to dribble their basketball continuously, staying within the cones. The chasers run in, trying to knock basketballs out of the area. If any participants lose control of their basketball and dribble outside the cones, they have to perform a skill or challenge (e.g., circle their basketball around the waist five times) before re-entering the working area. Count how many basketballs the chasers knock out in a set time, such as 45 to 60 seconds, and then change the chasers.

> ### Safety Tips
>
> ▶ Allow rest periods between games to allow participants to recover.
> ▶ Warn participants to be careful of collisions.

ADVICE

- Include more or fewer chasers depending on age and ability.
- This game is best for small groups. Split up larger groups so that there are two or more games running.
- Remind participants of the double-dribble rule (no bouncing with two hands or catching the basketball then starting to dribble again). If participants double-dribble they have to perform the skill or challenge.
- Teach the 'protected dribbling' technique. This technique involves dribbling with a low body position, protecting the ball by keeping the body between the opponent and the ball.

VARIATIONS

- **Game variation:** Any participants who have their basketballs knocked out of the area become chasers and the game continues until only one player is left with a basketball.

- **Game variation:** Dribblers have to move from one side of the coned area to the other as many times as possible in a minute without losing their basketball.

- **Game variation:** Play to the rules of *Catch and Release* (page 11). Any participants who have their basketballs knocked out of the area collect them and move back inside, holding onto their balls with their legs open. They are freed from this position if another participant dribbles their ball through their legs.

One-Hand Dribble   AGES 5-16

EQUIPMENT

One basketball each, cones.

GAME

This activity develops dribbling skills. Cone out your working area and give every participant a basketball. All participants have to continuously dribble their basketballs without letting other players knock them out of the area. Participants dribble the ball with either hand, but the spare hand should be used to knock other players' balls out of the area. Any participants who lose control of their basketball and dribble outside the cones have to perform a skill or challenge (e.g., circle their basketball around the waist five times) before re-entering the working area. Play for a set time, such as 2 minutes, and count how many times participants have their balls knocked out of the area.

> ### Safety Tips
>
> ▸ Warn participants to be careful of collisions.

ADVICE

- Remind participants of the double-dribble rule (no bouncing with two hands or catching the basketball then starting to dribble again). If participants double-dribble they have to perform the skill or challenge.

- Teach the 'protected dribbling' technique. This technique involves dribbling with a low body position, protecting the ball by keeping the body between the opponent and the ball.
- Encourage participants to knock away the basketball without making contact with the other player. If contact were made, this would constitute a *foul* in a match.
- Make the challenges fun for younger children. For older participants, the challenge could be to perform a basketball skill (e.g., score two baskets).

VARIATIONS

- **Harder:** Only allow the participants to dribble the basketball with a specific hand.
- **Harder:** Any participants who have their basketballs knocked out of the area become chasers. The game continues until only one player is left with a basketball.
- **Sport-specific:** This game can be adapted for other sports that involve dribbling skills (e.g., soccer or hockey).

Partner Shoot  AGES 5-16

EQUIPMENT

One basketball and basket between two and a stopwatch.

GAME

This activity develops shooting skills. Arrange the participants into pairs around each basket. Time the activity for 2 minutes. For the first minute one member of each pair becomes the shooter, while the other member acts as a rebounder. The shooter moves to a different position after each shot. The rebounder collects each shot and returns the basketball to the shooter. After the first minute, participants switch roles so that both players have a chance to shoot. Each pair combines the amount of baskets scored. The winning pair will have scored the most baskets at the end of the 2 minutes.

> ### Safety Tips
>
> ▶ If playing with more than one pair per basket, warn participants to be careful of collisions.

ADVICE

- You decide where the shooters take their shots from. For example, with experienced 15- and 16-year-olds you may say half of the shots have to be taken from outside the three-point line. For younger children you may state that all shots are taken within 5 m.
- Ensure the size of the basketballs are appropriate for participants' age and experience.
- With larger groups, have two or three pairs working into the same basket (however, see Safety Tips).

VARIATIONS

- **Game variation:** Mark out specific areas for participants to shoot from.
- **Game variation:** Time the participants to score 10 baskets (participants must score five baskets each).
- **Game variation:** Participants switch roles after each shot.
- **Harder:** Group participants in threes, adding a defender attempting to block the shooter when taking their shot.
- **Netball:** Play with the same rules as basketball.

Rebound

AGES 11-16

EQUIPMENT

One basketball and basketball backboard per 6 to 10 participants.

GAME

This activity develops rebounding skills. Arrange the participants into groups of 6 to 10. Each group should line up about 5 to 7 m away from the basket (see figure 2.2). The line should be half a metre to the side of the hoop. The first participant throws the ball up to hit the backboard so that it bounces back without hitting the hoop. The thrower jumps up and, while in mid-air, catches the ball and throws it back up against the backboard for the person behind to repeat the sequence. After each rebound, participants should land safely on the floor before joining the back of the line. The idea is to see how many times the participants can keep the sequence going.

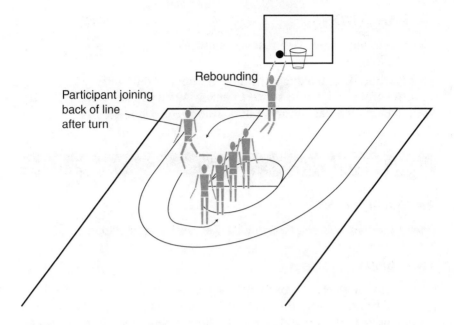

Rebounding

Participant joining
back of line
after turn

Figure 2.2

Safety Tips

▶ Allow rest periods for participants to recover.
▶ On landing, participants should quickly move to the back of the line.

● ADVICE

- Participants need to jump high so that they can have enough time to catch and throw before landing. This does not work well with less experienced or younger participants.
- Ensure the size of the basketballs and the height of the baskets are appropriate for participants' age and experience.
- Instruct participants to work cooperatively to keep the sequence going.
- It is not advisable to carry out this activity unless you have a basket that hangs away from the wall.

● *VARIATIONS*

- **Game variation:** Two teams compete to keep the sequence going the longest.
- **Harder:** After making a specified number of rebounds (e.g., 7 to 10) the group can try to score a basket. Again the shooter should try to catch the ball in the air and shoot before landing.

Sharpshooter  AGES 8-16

● *EQUIPMENT*

One basketball between two, one basket per four participants.

● *GAME*

In this shooting activity, participants try to score a basket before the person in front. Arrange the participants into groups of four. Each group should move to their own basket and line up behind the free-throw line (see figure 2.3). The front two participants each have a basketball. The first participant does the following:

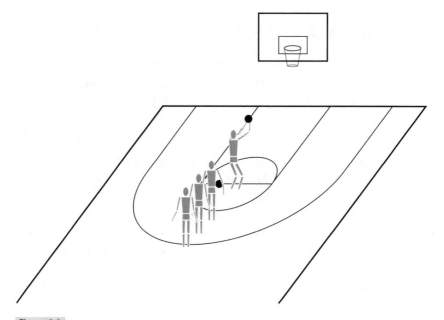

Figure 2.3

- He or she takes a shot from the free-throw line. If they miss, they then try as quickly as possible to score from anywhere they like.
- They can have as many shots as possible in their attempt to score.
- They try to score before the person behind them.

As soon as the first participant has taken their first shot, the second player can begin. Again they take their first shot from the free-throw line and then from anywhere they like. When any participant scores a basket, they pass the ball to the next person and join the back of the line.

Award each participant one point for each basket that is scored. Award two points if they score before the person in front of them. This sequence continues for a set time (e.g., 3 minutes). The participant with the most points at the end wins the game.

Safety Tips

▶ Warn participants to be careful of collisions.

ADVICE

- Ensure the size of the basketballs and the height of the baskets are appropriate for the participants' age and experience.
- Demonstrate the game when playing it with a group for the first time. The key concept for participants to understand is that to score two points they must score before the person in front of them. This is likely to happen if they score with their first shot when the person in front of them has missed theirs.
- Encourage players to dribble close to the hoop or take a lay-up for their second and subsequent shots.

VARIATIONS

- **Harder:** With more advanced participants, only allow them to shoot with their weaker hand.
- **Netball:** Use netball 'footwork' rules.

Stealer Basketball AGES 5-16

 EQUIPMENT

One basketball between two, cones.

 GAME

This is an activity that develops dribbling skills. Arrange the participants into groups of 8 to 12. Cone out a working area for each group. Within each group, half of the participants start with a basketball while the others begin without one. Participants with a basketball start by trying to dribble round the area continuously, while those who do not have one try to 'steal' one. If a basketball is stolen from a player dribbling, then the two participants switch roles. The participant with the ball tries to keep it, while the other participant tries to steal it. Inform participants that they may not steal a basketball from players that have just taken theirs. Play for a set time (e.g., 45 to 60 seconds) and see which participants have a ball at the end.

> **Safety Tips**
>
> ▶ Warn participants to be careful of collisions.

 ADVICE

- Remind participants of the double-dribble rule (no bouncing with two hands or catching the basketball then starting to dribble again). If participants double-dribble, they lose their basketball.

VARIATIONS

- **Easier/Harder:** Have more or fewer people in the group with a basketball to change the difficulty.
- **Harder:** Arrange each group into two teams of four to six. Each team has one to three basketballs. Participants from each team try to keep the basketball(s) they have and also steal their opponents' basketball(s). At the end of a set time count how many basketball(s) each team have to decide the winning team.

Team Shoot

 ### EQUIPMENT

One basketball per three to five participants, one basket per 6 to 10 participants, cones.

GAME

This activity develops shooting skills. Arrange the participants into teams of three to five. There should be two teams per basket. Cone out six shooting positions around each basket (see figure 2.4). The aim of the activity is for each team to score a basket from each of the shooting positions. Teams line up at opposite sides of the basket and the first participant in each team has a basketball. The first participant has a shot, collects his or her own rebound, passes the ball to the next player and joins the back of the line. This continues until any team member scores a basket. After a team member scores a basket, the whole team moves to the next shooting position and tries to score from there. The first team to score from each shooting position wins the game.

Figure 2.4

> ### Safety Tips
>
> ▸ Warn participants to be careful of collisions when rebounding their basketballs.
>
> ▸ Participants should be careful to avoid being hit by the opposing team's basketball.

☀ ADVICE

- The shooting positions' distance from the basket is dependant on age and ability.
- As teams move round they may need to shoot from a position that the opposing team is occupying. In this instance advise the group to miss out that particular position and go back to it when the opposing team has moved on.
- Smaller numbers in the groups means participants get more shots.

☀ VARIATIONS

- **Game variation:** Allow every team member to have a shot from each shooting position and count up the combined number of baskets scored by each team.
- **Game variation:** Allow participants a set time (e.g., 30 to 45 seconds) from each shooting position. Again count up the combined number of baskets scored by each team.
- **Harder:** As the participants improve, the amount of baskets scored from each position can be increased.
- **Harder:** Only shoot with the weaker hand.
- **Netball:** Play with the same rules as basketball.

Twenty-One   AGES 8-16

☀ EQUIPMENT

One basketball and basket per two or three participants.

GAME

This is an activity that develops shooting and rebounding skills. Arrange the participants into pairs or threes around each basket. Participants line up around 3 to 5 m from the basket. The front participant has a basketball. This person shoots then follows in for a rebound, trying to catch the basketball before it bounces. Irrespective of whether the first shot is scored or not, if the shooter catches the basketball before it bounces, they can attempt another shot. This must be taken from the spot where they caught the rebound. Participants take turns shooting from the starting point. It is possible to score either 3, 2, 1 or 0 points in the following ways:

- 3 points: A player scores with their first shot, takes the rebound before it bounces and scores with their second shot.
- 2 points: A player scores with their first shot but misses the second, or scores the first shot but does not take the rebound before it bounces.
- 1 point: A player misses their first shot but gets the rebound before the basketball bounces and scores with their second shot.
- 0 points: No baskets scored.

Participants must remember to keep their own score and the winner is the first to score 21 points.

ADVICE

- Ensure the size of the basketballs and the height of the baskets are appropriate for the participants' age and experience.
- Demonstrate the activity first so that all participants know how to score points.
- Advise participants to follow in for the rebound as soon as the first shot is taken.
- If time is limited, play for a smaller total (e.g., 15 points).

VARIATIONS

- **Easier/Harder:** Vary the distance of the first shot depending on age and ability.
- **Easier/Harder:** Participants themselves choose where they take the first shot.
- **Game variation:** Play for a set time (e.g., 3 minutes) with the winner being the participant with the highest total at the end.

- **Harder:** For more experienced players only, allow shots with the weaker hand.
- **Harder:** Play with an open rebound. This means that when one player shoots, their opponent stands next to them. As soon as the shot has been taken, both players can compete for the rebound to score the extra point.
- **Netball:** Play with the same rules as basketball.

Cricket,
Striking and
Fielding Games

The activities in this chapter relate to cricket and striking and fielding games. Collectively the activities develop batting, bowling and fielding skills. You can also adapt some of the activities for rounders, baseball or softball sessions. To find out whether an activity is suitable for other sports, consult the Variations section of each activity.

Four activities in the chapter are skill-based practices but have an element of competition to make them more challenging. The other six are activities that children really enjoy playing. These games have small recommended group sizes to ensure maximum participation. Many activities can also be played individually, allowing even more involvement.

The games introduce features of cricket such as overs, where one bowler bowls six balls in a row. Some games are structured in overs to familiarise participants with this concept.

Some children find cricket boring as the full game involves only a few players being active at one time. Therefore the activities included in this chapter require more participant involvement than the traditional game of cricket. This increases participants' enjoyment of the game and is more conductive to learning. For example in a cricket match, batters continue facing deliveries until they are out. This means that for the rest of the team there can be long periods of inactivity. Also once a batter is out, they do not get another chance to bat. To resolve these issues the games included here suggest that batters take turns to bat, or have shorter batting times.

When you use these activities in cricket sessions, use tennis balls with beginners or younger participants. For more able participants, use a cricket ball but have batters and wicketkeepers wear appropriate safety equipment. Bats should be a suitable size and weight for your participants. Throughout this chapter, we use the term 'wicket' to mean three stumps.

Beat the Fielder  AGES 5-16

● EQUIPMENT

One tennis ball per six participants, cones.

● GAME

This is an activity that develops fielding skills. Arrange the participants into groups of six, then split each group into two teams of three. Cone out a goal and a throwing line for each team (see figure 3.1). Between the throwing lines is an area called 'no man's land' that participants must not enter when they are throwing the ball or defending their goal. A partici- pant from team one starts by trying to throw the ball past team two to score a point. To do this the ball must pass through the goal below waist height. The opposing team tries to stop the ball going through the goal using fielding techniques. If team two catches the ball before it bounces, the catcher scores a point for their team. One of team two now attempts to throw the ball past team one. Participants take turns attempting to score points, alternating between teams, and the game continues for a set time (e.g., 3 to 4 minutes) or until one team scores a set number of points (e.g., 5 to 10).

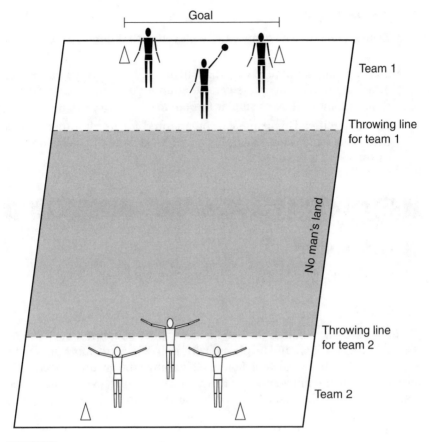

Figure 3.1

Safety Tips

▶ Ensure participants are suitably warmed up before playing the game, as it involves ballistic movements.

▶ Ensure participants do not throw in no man's land.

▶ The size of no man's land is dependant on age and experience. It should be challenging yet safe.

ADVICE

• When defending, the participants should stand with the middle participant in front of the other two. This is so that participants do not dive into each other when defending (see figure 3.1).

• Instruct the correct throwing, catching and fielding techniques.

VARIATIONS

- **Easier/Harder:** The game can be played with different numbers on a team.
- **Harder:** Instead of throwing the ball, it can be hit with a bat by the attacking team. The game can be adapted for hitting a variety of different shots. This is similar to *Beat the Fielder* (see page 66).
- **Sport-specific:** This game can be adapted for use in other sports using the same rules. Examples might be kicking the ball in soccer, or throwing it in softball.

Circuit Cricket   AGES **5-16**

EQUIPMENT

One tennis ball per 12 to 24 participants, four bats, four wickets.

GAME

This is a game well suited for use inside a sport hall, but it can also be played outdoors. It should be played with 12 to 24 participants per game. Set up the wickets as shown in figure 3.2. Arrange the group into teams of four, giving each team a letter. For example, four teams would be called teams A, B, C and D. Team A begins by batting and each member gets a bat and stands in front of a wicket. Those in team B become wicketkeepers and each member stands behind a wicket. The rest of the players become fielders standing anywhere except the centre area between the wickets. You stand in the centre of the area and bowl underarm to one of the batters. The batter tries to hit the ball away so that the team can score runs. To do this, the whole team must run to the next wicket, moving in an anti-clockwise direction.

When batting, participants are allowed to score more than one run per bowl by running to more than one wicket. Normal cricket rules apply when trying to get the batting team out. You always bowl to the same wicket. When a wicket is taken the whole team is out, so team B moves on to bat and team C to keep wicket. Teams A and D would field when team B is batting. The game continues until each team has had a specific number of innings (e.g., 2 to 4) or for a set time (e.g., 20 to 30 minutes).

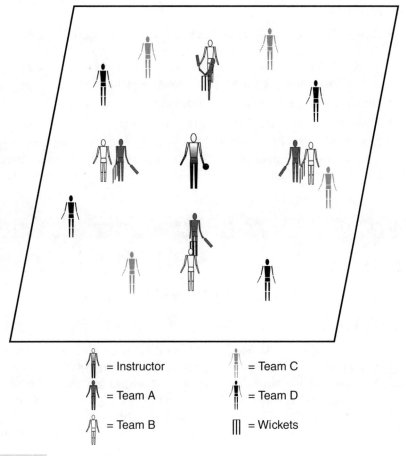

 = Instructor   = Team C

 = Team A   = Team D

 = Team B ||| = Wickets

Figure 3.2

Safety Tips

▶ Warn participants to be careful of collisions when fielding.

▶ Ensure the fielders stand at least 7 m away from the batter.

ADVICE

- Batters will need to communicate to score runs and avoid run-outs.
- Make sure a member from each team keeps their total of runs.

● *VARIATIONS*

- **Game variation:** Give each batting team an allocated number of deliveries or get the team to bat for a set time. Each team bats for all of the deliveries or for the full time but has three runs removed from their total each time a participant is given out.
- **Harder:** You can bowl to any of the wickets.
- **Harder:** Play *Tip and Run* rules (see page 86).
- **Rounders, softball, baseball:** This game can be modified for use in a rounders, softball or baseball session. This can be done by using bases instead of wickets and adapting the rules to suit the sport.

Drop, Bounce, Hit   AGES **5-16**

● *EQUIPMENT*

Six tennis balls and one wicket per four participants, cones.

● *GAME*

This activity is used to develop batting and fielding skills. The instructions given here are how to set the game up to work on the straight drive shot, but this activity can be adapted for use with other shots. Arrange the participants into groups of four and set up each group as shown in figure 3.3. Put a wicket where a batter and a feeder should stand. Place two cones 20 to 25 m away from the batters' wickets. The cones should be 8 to 10 m apart and form a target for the batter. Of the remaining participants one should stand in front of the target (the fielder) and the other should stand behind the target (the retriever). The fielder's job is to stop any balls hit by the batter from going through the target. The retriever collects any balls that have been hit past the fielder.

A ball is dropped in front of the batter, who tries to hit the ball through the target below head height to score a point. If the ball is hit in the air and the fielder catches it before it bounces then the batter loses a point. The batter is fed six balls and should keep score of how many shots are hit through the target. Rotate positions so that each participant has a chance to bat. Continue until all players have had three to five turns to bat.

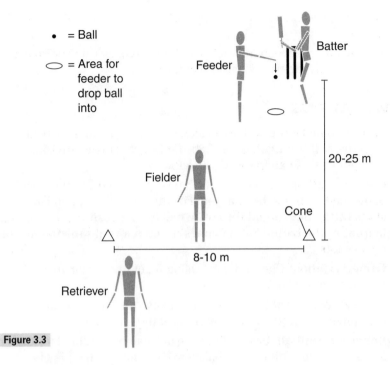

• = Ball

⬭ = Area for feeder to drop ball into

Batter

Feeder

20-25 m

Fielder

Cone

8-10 m

Retriever

Figure 3.3

Safety Tips

▶ Make sure the feeder is dropping the ball in front of the batter to avoid being hit by the bat during the batter's follow-through. It is vital that the feeder drops the ball and then moves his or her hand and arm out of the way.

▶ Make sure groups are not set up too close together to avoid participants being struck by stray hits from other groups. It helps if groups work away from the centre of the field. This also makes it easier to instruct the group.

▶ Make sure the feeder is in front of the batter (face to face; i.e., for a left-handed batter, the feeder and batter would stand opposite to what is shown in the diagram).

● ADVICE

• Change the size of the target area to suit the participants' age and ability. Make the area smaller to challenge the participants.

- Encourage participants to hit the ball along the floor rather than in the air.
- The distance between the wicket and the target can also be changed to suit the participants' age and ability.

VARIATIONS

- **Easier:** To make the activity easier, do not have a fielder trying to stop the ball from going through the target. This is advisable for younger or less experienced participants.
- **Game variation:** Different shots can be practised but the position of the feeder should be changed. For the hook, sweep, pull and cut shots the feeder should throw the ball from a position around 7 m in front of the batter. Set up cones in the relevant target areas for these shots.
- **Game variation:** Play in teams using a set-up similar to *Beat the Fielder* (see page 66).
- **Harder:** For more able participants, change the feed to an underarm then an overarm throw from in front of the batter.
- **Rounders, softball, baseball:** This game can be modified for use in a rounders, softball or baseball session. The ball feed is changed to a normal bowl and the targets will need to be slightly bigger.

Line and Length
AGES **8-16**

EQUIPMENT

Six hoops (chalk can be used as an alternative) and one tennis ball between two, one wicket each.

GAME

This is an activity used to develop accurate bowling techniques. Arrange the participants into pairs and give each pair a ball, two wickets and six hoops. The wickets and hoops should be set up as shown in figure 3.4. The wickets should be placed 22 yd (20.1 m) apart (21 yd [19.2 m] for under-thirteens, 20 yd [18.3 m] for under-twelves) as these are the regulation distances for a game of cricket. Three hoops should be placed on the ground 2, 4 and 6 m in front of each wicket. One participant starts by bowling at a set of hoops and a wicket. Their partner acts as a wicketkeeper standing behind the wicket. Before bowling, the participant must nominate which hoop they are aiming for. The bowler tries to hit this hoop and the wicket.

Participant 2

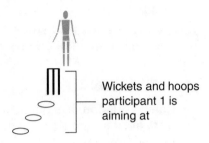

Wickets and hoops
participant 1 is
aiming at

Wickets and hoops
participant 2 is
aiming at

Participant 1

Figure 3.4

One point is awarded for hitting the nominated hoop, one for hitting the wicket and three if the participant hits the hoop and the wicket. After one bowl, participants swap roles so that the wicketkeeper bowls at the other wicket and the former bowler becomes the wicketkeeper. Participants take turns bowling and the winner of the game is the one who has scored the most points after taking a specific number of deliveries (e.g., 12), or the first person to reach a specific total (e.g., 15).

Safety Tips

▶ Make sure groups are not working too close together to avoid participants being hit by stray bowls from other groups.

▶ Make sure the hoops do not impede participants' follow-through after taking their turn to bowl.

✸ *ADVICE*

- Chalk could be used to draw out targets instead of hoops.
- Ensure bowlers bowl using correct techniques.
- The ball should land straight in the hoop to score. It should not bounce two or more times before hitting the nominated hoop.

✸ *VARIATIONS*

- **Game variation:** If equipment is limited, set up the participants to work in larger groups (e.g., three to five). Each group bowls at one wicket, taking turns to bowl and to be the wicketkeeper.
- **Game variation:** Play in teams of two or three. Participants take turns bowling, but points are added together to make a team total.
- **Harder:** Partners nominate which hoop to aim at.

Non-Stop Batting   AGES 5-16

✸ *EQUIPMENT*

One cricket bat, tennis ball and wicket per 10 to 14 participants, cones.

✸ *GAME*

This is a team game which develops batting and fielding skills. Set up the wicket and cones as shown in figure 3.5. The wicket should be placed on the ground and a cone should be placed on either side, 5 to 7 m away. Arrange participants into groups of 10 to 14, then split each group into two teams. One team starts batting, while the other team starts fielding. The fielding team nominates one participant to be the wicketkeeper, who stands behind the wicket. The rest of the team spreads out, trying to cover as much of the outfield as possible. Batters stand or sit behind the wicket well out of the way of the fielders. One of the batters steps up to the wicket to bat. You should do all the bowling from a coned area about 12 m from the wicket.

To start the game the ball should be delivered at the wicket with an underarm action. The batter tries to hit the ball away or defend by stopping the ball from hitting the wicket. *Whether batters hit the ball or not, they have to run around one of the side cones and back.* The batter tries to do this before the fielding team collects the ball and returns it to you to bowl again immediately. Every time batters get back to the wicket after running round one of the cones they score one run for their team. Bat-

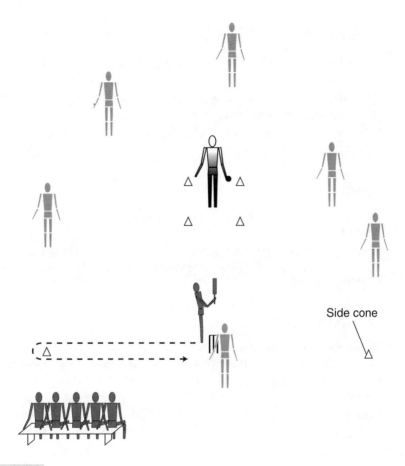

Figure 3.5

ters can score two or more runs each delivery by running round the two cones alternately. The fielding team tries to collect the ball and return it to you as quickly as possible. If the fielding team passes the ball to you before the batter gets back to the wicket, you may bowl at the wicket. This means there is a strong chance of bowling out the batter. The batter tries to score as many runs as possible until they are out. As well as being bowled out, batters can lose their wicket by being caught out or by hitting their own wicket with the bat. If the batter loses their wicket, he or she should sit down and the next batter steps up to bat.

A team's innings ends when all the batters have taken a turn to bat. At the end of an innings the teams swap roles, with the fielding team now batting and vice versa. Each team bats for a set number of innings (e.g., one to three), and the winning team is the one that scores the most runs.

> **Safety Tips**
>
> ▸ Ensure the fielders stand at least 7 m away from the batter.
>
> ▸ Fielders should not stand between the wickets and the cones as the batter may run into them.
>
> ▸ Warn the fielders to be careful of collisions when chasing the ball.

ADVICE

- With older or more experienced groups, one of the fielding team could bowl.

- It may be advisable to use a bigger target as the wicket (e.g., six stumps instead of three) so there is more chance of the bowler hitting the wicket.

VARIATIONS

- **Game variation:** Batters take a strike for six deliveries. If they are given out they do not sit down but lose three runs from the team's total. Each innings lasts until all the batters have taken their turn to bat.

- **Game variation:** If any batters are caught out, that is the end of their team's innings. This encourages batters to hit the ball low.

- **Small groups:** With smaller groups, participants can play individually by competing against the rest of the group. All participants field when they are not batting and try to beat the rest of the group by scoring the most runs.

- **Sport-specific:** This game can be adapted for use in soccer sessions. A larger target must be used for the wicket (e.g., five footballs placed on cones in a straight line). You kick the ball at the wicket and the batter tries to kick the ball away.

Play or Not   AGES 8-16

EQUIPMENT

One cricket bat, one tennis ball and two wickets per three participants, cones.

● *GAME*

This activity develops bowling and wicketkeeping techniques and good decision making while batting. Arrange the participants into groups of three. Each group should have two wickets, a ball, a bat and some cones. The wickets and cones should be set up as shown in figure 3.6. The wickets should be placed 22 yd (20.1 m) apart (21 yd [19.2 m] for under-thirteens, 20 yd [18.3 m] for under-twelves). Place the cones in a circle about 15 m in diameter around one of the wickets. One member of the group starts as a bowler, another becomes a batter, while the third acts as a wicketkeeper. While bowling, the aim is to bowl accurately at the wicket, forcing the batter to play a defensive shot. The batter tries to use judgement, leaving the balls that are not going to hit the wicket, and playing a defensive shot to block the balls that are. When playing such a shot, the ball should stop inside the circle of cones. The wicketkeeper

Figure 3.6

tries to stop any balls the bowler has delivered. The bowler will bowl one over (see chapter introduction) then switch with the wicketkeeper. This means the batter receives two overs (or 12 deliveries). The participants should each take a turn batting, receiving one over from the other two participants. Points can be scored and lost throughout the game and the participant with the most at the end wins.

Points are awarded while bowling and batting in the following ways:

- While bowling
  - Three points are awarded for forcing the batsman to play a defensive shot.
  - Five points are awarded for bowling the batter out.
  - One point is deducted for each wide bowl.
- While batting
  - One point is awarded for defending a ball with the ball stopping inside the circle of cones.
  - Three points are awarded for correctly leaving a ball that misses the wickets.
  - Five points are subtracted for being bowled out.

Safety Tips

▶ Ensure that groups are well spaced so participants aren't hit by stray balls from other groups.

ADVICE

- Participants should remember to keep scores.
- Batters do not score points if they decide to play a shot but miss the ball, even if the ball doesn't hit the wicket.
- Ensure participants bowl with correct bowling techniques.

VARIATIONS

- **Harder:** This can be adapted into a team game. Score using the usual rules of cricket, but add an extra point for bowlers forcing the batter to play a defensive shot, and an extra point for batters correctly defending a ball that would have hit the wicket.
- **Large groups:** With larger groups, have more participants bowling.

Score the Single AGES **5-16**

EQUIPMENT

Cricket bats, tennis balls and wickets.

GAME

This is a team game which develops batting and fielding skills. Set up the wickets and cones as shown in figure 3.7. The wickets should be placed so that there is a distance of about 20 m between them. Arrange participants into two teams of six or seven at most. One team starts as batters, while the other team starts as fielders. The fielding team nominates one person to be the wicketkeeper, who stands behind the wicket. The rest of the team spreads out, trying to cover as much of the outfield as possible. Batters stand behind the wicket well out of the way of the fielders. One of the batters steps up to the wicket to bat. You do all the bowling,

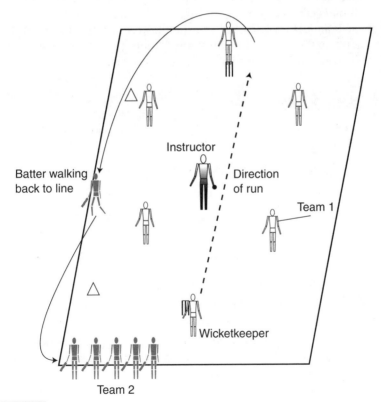

Figure 3.7

standing between the wickets about 12 m away from the batter. To start the game the ball is delivered at the wicket with an underarm action. The batter tries to hit the ball away or defend by stopping the ball from hitting the wicket. *Whether the batter hits the ball or not, they have to run.* They must run to the other wicket, and thus 'score the single'. The fielding team try to prevent the batter scoring the single by collecting the ball and throwing it at the wicket to which the batter is running. If the batter gets to that wicket before the fielding team hits it, a point is added to his or her team total. If a fielder hits the wicket before the batter gets there then the batter is 'run out'. If a batter is run out he or she loses two points from their team's total.

Regardless of whether batters score a point or are run out, they walk back to the line and wait for their next turn to bat. They should be kept out of the way by cones down the side of the playing area. As well as being run out batters can lose their wicket by being bowled out, caught out or by hitting their own wicket with the bat. Again two points are taken off the team's total for being out. Batters take turns to face a delivery and their innings continues until each batter has had a set number of deliveries (e.g., 3 balls each) or for a set time (e.g., 5 minutes). At the end of an innings the teams swap roles, with the fielding team now batting and vice versa. Each team bats for a set number of innings (e.g., one to three), and the winning team is the one that scores the most runs.

Safety Tips

▸ Ensure the fielders stand at least 7 m away from the batter.

▸ Fielders should not stand between the wickets as the batter may run into them.

▸ Warn the fielders to be careful of collisions when chasing the ball.

ADVICE

- Ensure batters run even if they miss the ball.
- Fielders can rotate positions every six deliveries so that they all get a chance to be the wicketkeeper.
- With older or more experienced participants, this game is best played in a sport hall as better batters will hit the ball further outdoors, making the game too easy.

VARIATIONS

- **Game variation:** Allow the fielders to bowl for themselves. With older or more experienced participants, make the bowlers deliver using an overarm action.

- **Harder:** Allow the batter to score more than one run per delivery by running back and forth between the wickets.

- **Harder:** Change the rules so that in any one innings, batters are not allowed to bat again if they are out. In this instance an innings should be timed or the team should be given a set number of deliveries (e.g., 18 to 24). If all the batters are out before the end of this time or number of deliveries, the teams switch roles.

- **Rounders, softball, baseball:** This game can be modified for use in a rounders, softball or baseball session using similar rules.

Take Away Five   AGES 11-16

EQUIPMENT

Two cricket bats, one tennis ball and two wickets per six participants.

GAME

This is a modified game of cricket where participants work in pairs against the rest of their group. It develops all the skills found in the full game of cricket. Arrange the participants into groups of six and ask them to work with a partner within their group. Partners work together throughout the game trying to score as many runs as possible in order to beat the other pairs. Each group should have two wickets, two bats and a ball. The wickets should be placed 22 yd (20.1 m) apart (21 yd [19.2 m] for under-thirteens, 20 yd [18.3 m] for under-twelves). One pair in the group starts as batters. Of the rest of the participants, one bowls, one keeps wicket and the other two field (see figure 3.8). The batters will bat for four overs with each pair taking a chance to bat (see chapter introduction). Therefore, each of the other participants will bowl one over at the batters. Points can be scored and lost throughout the game and the pair with the most points at the end wins. If a batting pair are out they continue to bat, but five points are taken away from their total, hence the name of the game.

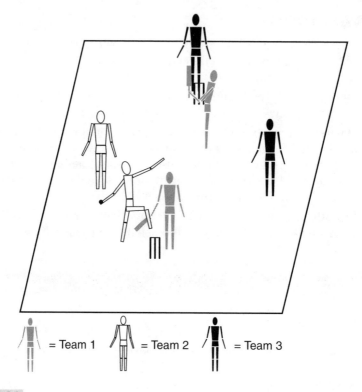

Figure 3.8

Points are awarded while bowling, batting and fielding in the following ways:

- While bowling
    - Two points are deducted for bowling a wide or no-ball.
    - Five points are awarded if a batter loses their wicket by being bowled out, caught out, hitting the wicket, hitting the ball twice or being stumped.
    - Ten points are awarded for taking a 'caught and bowled' wicket. This is when the bowler catches the ball without it bouncing after the batter hits it.
- While batting
    - One point is awarded for each run scored.
    - Two points are awarded for a wide bowl or no-ball (in this game no extra ball is delivered).

- Five points are subtracted for getting out. In addition to being run out, batters can be out by any of the ways previously listed.
- Boundary fours and sixes can be awarded if groups have designated boundaries.
- While fielding
  - Five points are awarded for taking a catch. This means catching the ball without it bouncing after the batter has hit it.

Safety Tips

▶ Ensure the fielders stand at least 7 m away from the batter.

▶ Warn the fielders to be careful of collisions when chasing the ball.

ADVICE

- Set up wickets closer together if working with younger or less experienced participants.
- Encourage the groups to work quickly between deliveries to maximise playing time.

VARIATIONS

- **Easier:** You can bowl underarm to younger participants.
- **Large groups:** This game can be played in groups of eight. If time is limited, reduce the number of deliveries bowled by the other six participants.

Throw and Back Up
AGES 8-16

EQUIPMENT

One cricket bat and tennis ball per six to seven participants, two wickets per group, cones.

● GAME

This is a modified game of cricket with an emphasis placed on developing fielding techniques. Set up the wickets and cones as shown in figure 3.9. The wickets should be placed approximately 22 yd (20.1 m) apart (21 yd [19.2 m] for under-thirteens, 20 yd [18.3 m] for under-twelves). Around the wickets, cones should be placed on the floor making circles, each 8 m in diameter. Arrange the participants into two teams of six to seven at most. One team starts as batters, while the other team begins as fielders. The fielding team nominates one participant to bowl and one to be the wicketkeeper. The wicketkeeper stands behind the wicket but outside the circle of cones. The rest of the team spreads out, trying to cover as much of the outfield as possible. Batters line up behind the wicket well out of the way of the fielders.

Batters take turns facing a delivery. Fielders take turns to bowl, each of them bowling at three batters in a row. The batter tries to hit the ball away or play a defensive shot to stop the ball from hitting the wicket. *Whether the batter hits the ball or not, they have to run.* They must run continuously between the wickets until the fielders run them out or they

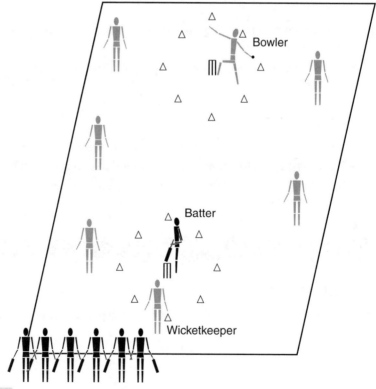

Figure 3.9

have scored four runs. The fielders try to prevent the batter scoring by collecting the ball and throwing it at the wicket. The fielders must throw from outside the coned areas. If the batter plays the ball into either coned area, the fielders have to retrieve the ball from inside and either pass or run the ball out before they can throw at the wicket. Participants should 'back up', which means that when a fielder picks the ball up and is about to throw it at the wicket, team-mates stand in a position to stop the ball if it misses. When batters are run out, the amount of runs they have scored is added to the team's total. It is possible to score either 0, 1, 2, 3 or 4 depending on how quickly the fielders hit the wicket.

After their turn batters join the back of the line and wait for their next turn. As well as being run out, batters can lose their wicket by being bowled, caught out or hitting their own wicket with the bat. In this instance they score no runs. The batting team continues its innings until each batter has had a set number of deliveries (e.g., three balls each) or for a set time (e.g., 10 minutes). When an innings ends the teams swap roles, with the fielding team now batting and vice versa. Each team bats for a set number of innings (e.g., one to three). The team scoring the most runs at the end of the four innings wins the game.

Safety Tips

▷ Ensure the fielders stand at least 7 m away from the batter.

▷ Warn the fielders to be careful of collisions when chasing the ball.

● ADVICE

- The batter can be run out by hitting either wicket. It doesn't have to be the wicket at the end the batter is running to.
- Make the diameter of the coned circle bigger or smaller depending on participants' age and experience.
- Ensure batters run even if they miss the ball.
- Fielders can rotate positions every three deliveries so that they move quickly between positions.

● VARIATIONS

- **Easier:** You can bowl underarm for younger participants.
- **Game variation:** Fielders can enter the coned areas to hit the wickets after a specified number of throws (e.g., three attempts).

- **Harder:** Specify that fielders must use underarm or overarm throwing techniques when trying to hit the wicket.
- **Small groups:** With smaller groups participants can play individually by competing against the rest of the group. All participants field when they are not batting. Participants try to beat the rest of the group by scoring the most runs.

Tip and Run

 EQUIPMENT

One cricket bat, one tennis ball and two wickets per 6 to 10 participants.

 GAME

This is a modified game of cricket with an emphasis placed on developing quick fielding techniques and good running between the wickets. Normal rules of cricket apply except that this is a paired competition instead of a team game, and there is a 'tip and run' rule. The rule is that *batters must run if they hit the ball with their bat.* Arrange the participants into groups of 6, 8 or 10 and ask them to work with a partner within their group. Partners work together throughout the game, trying to score as many runs as possible in order to beat the other pairs. Each group should have two wickets, two bats and a ball. The wickets should be placed approximately 22 yd (20.1 m) apart (21 yd [19.2 m] for under-thirteens, 20 yd [18.3 m] for under-twelves). One pair starts as batters. Of the rest of the participants one bowls, one keeps wicket and the others field (see figure 3.10). The batters will bat until one of them is out or they have faced an over from the rest of the group (see chapter introduction). Batters can be given out by being run out, stumped, caught out, bowled out or hitting their wicket. Each pair has two innings. The pair scoring the most runs at the end of the game wins.

> **Safety Tips**
>
> ▶ Ensure the fielders stand at least 7 m away from the batter.
> ▶ Warn the fielders to be careful of collisions when chasing the ball.

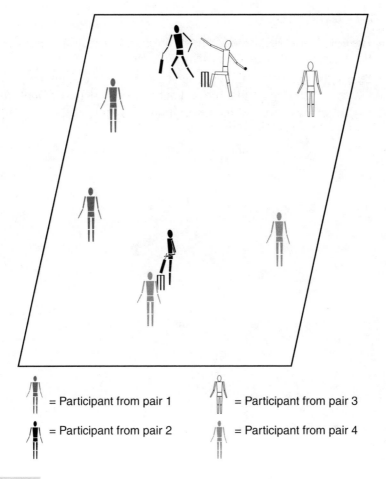

= Participant from pair 1

= Participant from pair 2

= Participant from pair 3

= Participant from pair 4

Figure 3.10

ADVICE

- Instruct batters to play the ball into spaces away from the fielders.
- For a no-ball or wide ball, the batters are awarded two runs but no extra ball.
- Fielders can rotate positions to ensure quick movement between the overs.

VARIATIONS

- **Harder:** If batters are out, they continue but lose five runs from their total (similar to *Take Away Five,* page 81).

- **Small groups:** With smaller groups participants can play individually by competing against the rest of the group. All participants field when they are not batting. Participants try to beat the rest of the group by scoring the most runs.

Hockey
Games

The activities in this chapter relate to hockey. Collectively the activities develop shooting, dribbling, passing and receiving skills. Most activities require minimal equipment apart from hockey sticks and balls.

It is possible to use most of the activities with indoor equipment in a gym or sports hall. If playing outdoors the ideal surface for these activities is an 'Astroturf' or artificial surface. Most activities can be carried out on grass.

For safety reasons, when instructing younger participants, use mini-hockey balls and smaller sticks. All participants should wear shin-guards for protection. Some activities require a goalkeeper. If you do use a goalkeeper then they must wear full safety equipment. This equipment is expensive and time-consuming to put on. For this reason it is not always practical to have goalkeepers. Where an activity suggests you use a goalkeeper, alternative options are provided so that everyone can take part. This information is found in the Variations section of each activity. Many of the hockey activities can be adapted for use with other invasion games.

Best out of Nine AGES 8-16

EQUIPMENT

Cones, two goals per 10 participants, one hockey stick and ball each, one set of goalkeeper's equipment per five participants.

GAME

This is an activity which develops dribbling, shooting and defending skills. Arrange the participants into groups of 10. Each group should have two goals and cones set up as shown in figure 4.1. They should work in two lanes approximately 20 m long and 10 m wide. Place the goals at opposite ends with one in each lane. At the opposite end to each of the goals, place cones on the ground to indicate starting positions for an attacker and a defender. Nominate two participants from each group to start as goalkeepers. The remaining participants work in pairs. Within each pair, participants compete against each other. They take turns to attack and defend by switching roles when working in each lane. The attacker starts with the ball on the left of the lane, slightly ahead of the defender. The defender has three starting positions and the attacker decides which position the defender starts at. The further back the attacker makes the defender stand, the easier it should be to score.

Shout 'Go!' The attacker dribbles toward the goal, trying to score past the keeper. The defender chases the attacker and tries to stop him or her scoring by making a tackle, hitting the ball out of the lane or blocking the shot. After each attack participants move to the next lane and switch roles. A point is awarded to the attacker if he or she scores, but a point is awarded to the defender if a goal is not scored. The pairs have nine attempts and the winner is the participant who scores the most points (i.e., scores the 'best out of nine'). When all the pairs have finished, change the goalkeepers and the remaining participants work with a new partner.

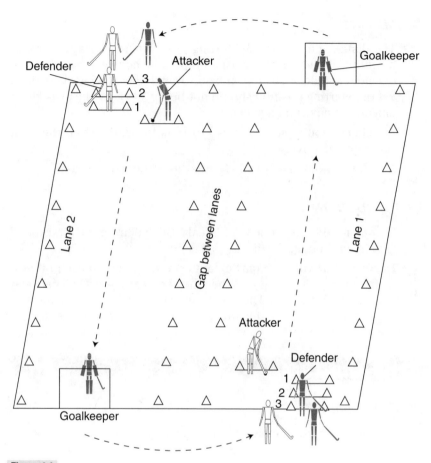

Figure 4.1

Safety Tips

▶ Warn participants to be careful of collisions.

▶ Ensure goalkeepers wear suitable safety equipment.

▶ Ensure there is a gap between the lanes.

▶ Ensure the attacker and defender move out of the way quickly. They must not stand behind the goal when they are waiting for their turn, as they may get hit by stray shots from other groups.

▶ Have defenders on the right-hand side of the lanes so that they are less likely to trip the attackers while tackling them.

● *ADVICE*

- The distance between the starting positions for the attacker and defender should ensure there is competition between the pairs. The defender should not be too far back to catch the attacker every time. Yet the starting position should not be too close or the attacker is unlikely to have much success.
- Attackers should play the ball 5 to 10 m forward so that they can run more effectively.
- Attackers should aim to shoot into the corners of the goal.

● *VARIATIONS*

- **Game variation:** If a defender 'steals' the ball from the attacker or gets to a rebound, a strike at goal is permitted.
- **Harder:** Start with the participants standing next to each other a metre apart facing the goal. When they are ready, roll a ball between them towards the goal. The participants race to the ball with the first to get there becoming the attacker, and the other one defending.

Flip and Turn   AGES **8-13**

● *EQUIPMENT*

Coloured cones (approximately 10 of each colour in three different colours), one hockey ball and stick each, approximately 10 mini-hurdles.

● *GAME*

This activity develops dribbling techniques and can be used as a skills practice or as part of a progressive warm-up. The whole group can be involved in the same area, or smaller groups can be set up using smaller areas. Using one of the sets of coloured cones, mark out your working area. Scatter the remaining cones and hurdles inside this area. You might use white cones to mark out the boundary, with red and blue cones scattered inside. Participants each have a hockey stick that they use to dribble a ball around the area. If participants dribble to a blue cone, they must move their ball around it clockwise before continuing. If they dribble to a red cone then they must go around it anti-clockwise before moving off again. When participants come across a hurdle, they attempt to flick their ball over the hurdle before dribbling off again.

Safety Tips

▶ Warn participants to be careful of collisions.

▶ Advise participants to keep looking up between touches.

▶ Participants must not try to lift their ball over the hurdle if there is another player on the other side of it. The ball should just pass over the hurdle and not go too high.

▶ Ensure there is plenty of space in the area so that cones and hurdles are not close together.

ADVICE

• To flick the ball, participants need to stop the ball and roll it back toward themselves so that they can get their hockey stick underneath.

• Change the size of the hurdles to be suitable for the age and ability of the group. Taller hurdles are more difficult to flick the ball over.

VARIATIONS

• **Easier/Harder:** Change the commands when encountering the obstacles. Examples could be turning away from the obstacle or pushing the ball round one side of an obstacle while running round the other side.

• **Invasion games:** This can be adapted for use in other sports that involve dribbling such as soccer and basketball. For example, participants could dribble soccer balls.

Horses and Jockeys   AGES 5-16

EQUIPMENT

One hockey ball between two, one hockey stick each.

GAME

This activity develops dribbling skills. See figure 4.2 for the set-up of this activity. Arrange the participants into pairs. Participants stand in a large

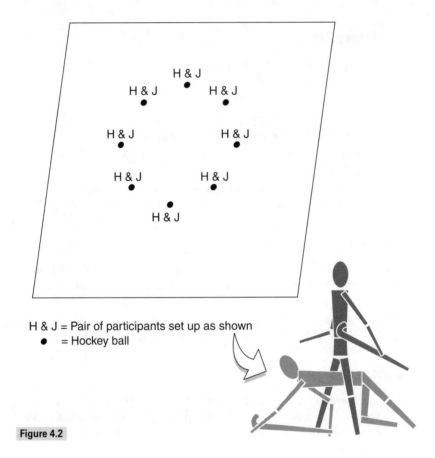

H & J = Pair of participants set up as shown
● = Hockey ball

Figure 4.2

circle. Each participant should have a hockey stick and each pair should have a hockey ball. Instruct the pairs to 'saddle up'. This is where one participant acts as the 'horse' while their partner acts as the 'jockey'. The horses get onto their hands and knees (with their head towards the centre of the circle). The jockeys stand over the horses, again facing the centre. The balls should be placed to the side of each pair (see figure 4.2). Call out either 'horse' or 'jockey'. If 'horse' is called, all horses stand up, then race around the circle dribbling their ball. They should all go anti-clockwise around the outside and should finish in the saddle up position. If 'jockey' is called, then the jockeys race in the same way. Award points for the first three pairs back in the saddle up position (e.g., 3, 2 and 1 points for the 1st, 2nd and 3rd pairs, respectively). After each participant has raced five times, the pair with the most points wins the game.

Safety Tips

► Ensure the jockey does not sit on the horse as this may cause back injuries.

► Ensure participants dribbling the ball do not trip over or dribble into those who are left standing in the circle.

► The surface should not be slippery as participants are likely to slide if they are moving fast.

ADVICE

- There are a number of variations of this activity as detailed under Variations, so try to change the game frequently to maintain interest.

- Allow rest periods so that participants have a chance to recover.

- If the ground is wet and chilly, get the horse to crouch without putting their hands down to avoid getting too cold.

- Advise participants to stay close to the circle when dribbling. The further out they go, the further they run, which takes longer.

VARIATIONS

- **Game variation:** Participants can dribble round the circle in a clockwise direction.

- **Game variation:** Participants must crawl through their partner's legs before dribbling.

- **Game variation:** Participants must run around their partner before dribbling.

- **Game variation:** Place the balls in the centre. Participants must collect a hockey ball and dribble it through the space to their partner's right before doing a lap of the circle.

- **Invasion games:** This game can be adapted for use in other sports that involve dribbling such as soccer and basketball. For example, participants dribble a soccer ball round the circle.

Score to Run Out   AGES 8-13

EQUIPMENT

Cones, one hockey ball and goal per 10 participants, one hockey stick each.

🌑 *GAME*

Use this activity to develop hitting, shooting, passing and teamwork. Arrange the participants into groups of 10, then split each group into two teams of five. Each participant should have a hockey stick. Set up the groups as shown in figure 4.3. Nominate one team to field, while the opposing team starts as batters. The fielders try to position themselves so that they cover as much of the outfield as possible. Of the batters, one participant stands in front of the goal while the rest stand beside it. The participant in front of the goal is the 'striking batter', whose role is to hit the hockey ball away, like a batter in rounders or softball.

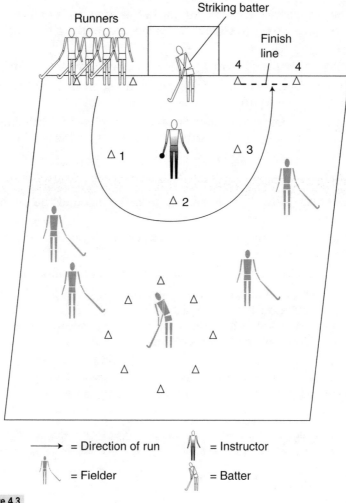

Figure 4.3

Put out three cones, which the batting team have to run around. This is similar to a baseball or softball diamond. Place a fourth cone as the last base in a straight line from the third base, well out of the way of the goal. This should ensure no batters are hit by stray shots from their opponents. Further from the goal, mark out a circle of cones approximately 10 m in diameter.

Stand between the goal and second base and roll the ball to the striking batter. The rest of the batting team are 'runners' who must try to race round the diamond after the striking batter has hit the ball. They all run together and try to complete one lap as fast as possible, including the striking batter.

The fielders try to retrieve the ball as quickly as they can and score a goal before the runners finish. However, before they can shoot they must play the ball into the circle of cones. Here three members of the team must touch the ball, by passing to each other, before attempting to score. They must take the shot from inside the diamond, so the ball must be passed into this area after the touches are made. The batting team score a run if any runners complete the lap before the fielders score a goal. If all the runners finish the lap, they score five runs. Therefore, the fielding team try to make the passes in the circle then score before any of the runners complete their lap.

A batting team completes one inning when each member has taken a turn as the striking batter. At the end of the inning add up all runs to give the team total. Teams then switch roles, with the batting team now fielding and vice versa. Each team has a set number of innings (e.g., 2 to 5), and the team scoring the most runs at the end of this wins the game.

Safety Tips

▶ The fielding team must not pass the ball into the circle if it is likely to hit the runners. They must use teamwork to pass the ball around and into the circle. The runners must keep glancing at the ball to ensure they are not hit by stray passes.

▶ You and the striking batter must move out of the way of the goal so that the fielding team have a clear shot at the target.

▶ Ensure the fielders stand well back from the striking batter.

● ADVICE

- You may need to change the number of passes the fielding team has to make before shooting, depending on how quickly the runners can run.
- If goals are not available, use cones instead.

● VARIATIONS

- **Game variation:** The striking batter runs after hitting the shot. The rest of the team do not and wait their turn at the side.
- **Harder:** Select one of the batting team to be a goalkeeper. Make sure they wear full protective clothing.
- **Sport-specific:** This game can be adapted for use in soccer using similar rules.

Speed Shot   AGES 8-16

● EQUIPMENT

One goal per four participants, one hockey stick each, at least one hockey ball each.

● GAME

This is a shooting activity that can be used to develop a good backswing and follow-through when striking the ball. This enables participants to learn how to shoot the ball powerfully. Arrange the participants into groups of four and set up each group as shown in figure 4.4. Each group should have four to six hockey balls and a goal. Nominate one shooter and three ball collectors in each group. The ball collectors stand behind the goal ready to stop any balls that are shot wide by the shooter. The shooter stands 8 to 12 m in front of the goal and positions the hockey balls in a straight line on the floor. They should all be about 30 cm apart, on the shooter's right. The shooter takes a backswing then swings the hockey stick forward and strikes all the balls in turn. The shooter should swing the hockey stick back and forth, taking a step toward the next ball with each backswing. The hockey stick should swing in a pendulum motion and there should be no pause between shots. After the hockey balls have been shot, the ball collectors return the balls, then participants rotate positions. Each participant should have three to five turns shooting the balls. They should count the amount of goals scored and after they have all had the required amount of shots, the person scoring the most wins the game.

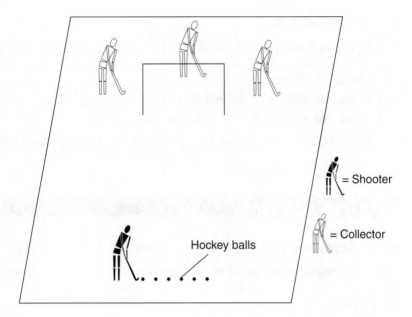

Figure 4.4

Safety Tips

▶ Ensure groups are not working close to others to avoid participants being hit by stray shots from other groups.

▶ Participants should keep a safe distance from the striker during the shooting activity.

▶ Ball collectors should stand well back from the goal and keep their eye on all the shots.

ADVICE

- If participants are older or more experienced they should shoot from a greater distance (e.g., 10 to 12 m).
- Shots should be steady, not rushed, to encourage balance and precision.
- Encourage participants to keep their heads down when striking each ball.
- This activity is best carried out with a fence close behind the goal so that missed shots do not travel far. Ball collectors should stand out of the way until all shots have been taken.

VARIATIONS

- **Game variation:** Cones can be used for goals. You could also have participants working in pairs hitting through the cones from one side to the other side.
- **Game variation:** Use more balls in the line.
- **Game variation:** Shoot from a different angle.
- **Harder:** Add a goalkeeper, but ensure correct safety equipment is worn.

Traffic Control   AGES 5-10

EQUIPMENT

Cones, one hockey ball and hockey stick each.

GAME

Use this activity as part of a progressive warm-up and to help develop dribbling skills. Cone out your working area. Participants each have a hockey stick and ball. They dribble their ball round the area in different directions, slowly building up speed.

Once the participants are moving round, call out one of the following 'traffic controls' and players must respond accordingly:

- 'Red'—participants stop with their ball.
- 'Amber'—participants tap their ball from left to right while standing still.
- 'Green'—participants dribble their ball round the area.
- 'Highway'—participants speed up.
- 'Reverse'—participants dribble their ball backwards.
- 'Dangerous driver'—you run into the area with a hockey stick and try to hit the participants' balls out of the coned area. If a ball is hit out, the participant performs a fun challenge before rejoining the game.

Safety Tips

▸ If used as part of a warm-up, ensure movements are progressive. Begin with less intense movements, adding more vigorous actions towards the end.

▸ Warn participants to be careful of collisions.

▸ Ensure the size of the area is large enough for the participants to move around in.

⬤ ADVICE

- Add one command at a time, as the participants may not remember all of the actions if you say them all at the start.

- Encourage participants to keep close control of their ball and to frequently look up so that they do not dribble into other players.

⬤ VARIATIONS

- **Harder:** Hold up a red, yellow or green cone for the red, amber or green commands, respectively.

- **Invasion games:** This game can be adapted for use in other sports which involve dribbling, such as soccer and basketball.

Winner Stays On   AGES 14-16

⬤ EQUIPMENT

Bibs in three different colours, cones, one hockey stick and hockey ball each, one goal and one set of goalkeeping equipment per 10 participants.

⬤ GAME

This is a shooting and finishing activity that can be used to develop quick attacking play as well as defending skills. See figure 4.5 for the set-up of this activity. Arrange the participants into groups of 10. In each group there should be one goalkeeper and three teams of three participants. Each team should put a different-coloured bib on. For example, you may have one team wearing blue bibs, one wearing red and one wearing yellow. The working area for this activity is the shooting D. The goalkeeper stands in goal and two of the teams stand in the shooting D. Three cones are placed

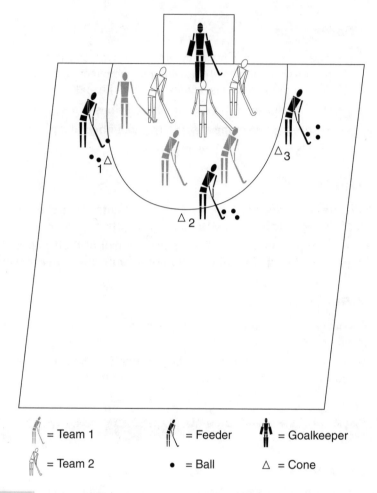

Figure 4.5

on the floor just outside the D and given numbers one, two and three. The participants from the remaining team each stand by one of the numbered cones and become 'feeders'. They should have three hockey balls each. Start the game by calling out the number of a cone. The participant standing at that cone rolls a hockey ball into the D. The two teams inside the D compete against each other to score past the goalkeeper. If one player shoots, any participant can follow in for the rebound.

As soon as the ball goes out of play (either into the goal or out of the D), call for another hockey ball to be played into the D. The game continues until all nine hockey balls have been played into the D. At this point the team scoring the most points stays on to play the team who was 'feeding' during the last game. Those in the losing team now move on to be the feeders.

ADVICE

- If playing for longer than 10 minutes, use the rotation version (see Variations) to allow recovery periods.

- Make sure a number is called as soon as a ball has gone out of play or a goal has been scored.

- If the score is tied after a game, the team who has been on the longest becomes the feeders.

VARIATIONS

- **Easier:** This game can be played without goalkeepers, using the same rules.

- **Game variation:** Rotation version: instead of playing so that the winning team stays on, rotate the teams so that each has a turn being the feeders.

- **Harder:** Separate into four teams, but play with three teams in the D.

Zigzag Pass

AGES **5-16**

EQUIPMENT

Cones, one hockey ball per three to five participants, one hockey stick each.

GAME

Use this activity as part of a progressive warm-up, a skills practice or as a competitive race to develop passing skills. Arrange the participants into teams of three to five. All the participants need a hockey stick and each team should have a ball. Each team works in their own 'lane', which is approximately 40 to 50 m long and 5 m wide. There should be a 5-metre gap between each lane. Each team forms 'mini-gates' down the sides of their lane by placing two cones 1 m apart on the floor. Between each mini-gate there should be a 4-metre gap. On one side, place the first mini-gate at the beginning of the lane. On the other side, place the first mini-gate after a 3-metre gap (see figure 4.6). Participants should stand in the first few mini-gates, with the person at the start having the ball. Start the activity by calling 'Go!' The participants pass the ball across their lane to each mini-gate in a zigzag pattern. After passing the ball, participants must move to the next free mini-gate so that this sequence can continue. The team that gets their ball to the end of the lane first wins.

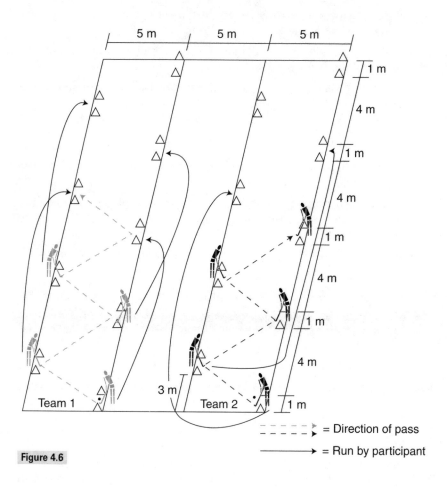

Figure 4.6

ADVICE

- If there are three or five in each team, ensure participants run behind the person they have passed to in order to get to the next available mini-gate. If there are four in the team, participants should run along the same side of the lane (see figure 4.6).

VARIATIONS

- **Easier/Harder:** Change the distance between the passer and receiver.
- **Harder:** The ball must travel up and down the lane before the game is won.
- **Harder:** Two or more balls can be introduced. With more added, the team sizes need to be bigger.
- **Harder:** Try reverse-stick passes.
- **Striking/fielding/invasion games:** This game can be adapted to various other sports which involve throwing and catching or passing.

Zone Attack  AGES 8-16

EQUIPMENT

One bib between two, one hockey stick each, one hockey ball per 10 participants, cones.

GAME

Use this activity to develop passing and support as well as defending skills. It is played using similar rules to a normal hockey match but instead of scoring into goals, participants must pass the ball into 'target zones' to score. For the set-up of this activity see figure 4.7. Arrange the participants into groups of 10, and separate each group into two teams

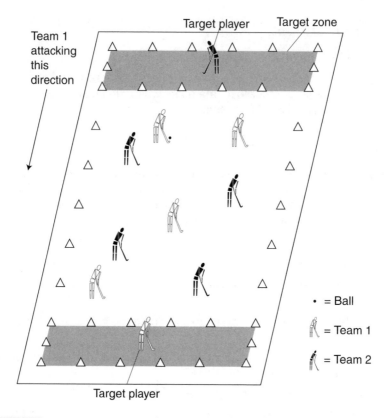

Team 1
attacking
this
direction

Target player   Target zone

• = Ball

ᛮ = Team 1

ᛮ = Team 2

Target player

Figure 4.7

of five. One team in each group puts bibs on. For each group, cone out a
large rectangular pitch. At each of the two shorter sides, set out target
zones. These are the scoring areas. The target zones should be about 5 m
in length. Teams attack the opposite target zones, and members nominate
which areas they are attacking. A 'target player' from each team stands in
their target zone. No other players are allowed to enter this zone, whereas
the target player must stay inside it.

One of the teams starts with the ball in front of the target zone they
are defending (containing their opponents' target player). When the
game begins the team in possession must try to pass the ball up to their
own target player. If this is achieved and the target player controls the
ball, stopping it within the target zone, a point is scored. The opposing
team works to stop the ball being passed through to the target zone it
is defending. If the defending team takes the ball from the other, it can
try to score by passing to its own target player. After a point has been
scored, both target players should be changed. Participants all move

back to their defending half of the pitch and the team that has conceded the point restarts with possession of the ball. Play for a set time (e.g., 5 to 10 minutes) or until one team has scored a set number of points, such as 10.

> ## Safety Tips
>
> ▸ Warn participants to be careful of collisions.
>
> ▸ Ensure participants are not trying to power shots through areas where opponents are standing to get the ball to the target player. Team members should dribble around opponents or pass through the gaps left by them to score points.
>
> ▸ Ensure there is a space left between pitches so that participants do not run onto other pitches while moving down the side of their own.

● ADVICE

- Advise the target player that they are allowed to move around inside the target zone. This should assist movement into space and help them to receive passes from team-mates.
- As the participants become more able, make the target area smaller to increase the difficulty.

● VARIATIONS

- **Easier/Harder:** Change the numbers of outfield players or target players on each team.
- **Game variation:** Do not have a target player. To score, any participant can run into the target zone to receive a pass.
- **Game variation:** Do not have a target player. Participants score by dribbling the ball into the target zone and stopping the ball. This switches the emphasis from a passing to a dribbling game.
- **Harder:** To make the game more difficult, team members must all have received a pass before the ball is played through to the target player.

Parachute
Games

This games in this chapter relate to using a parachute. Parachute activities work best with under-elevens. The activities usually need a minimum of 10 participants, depending on the size of the parachute. With larger parachutes it is possible to accommodate up to 30 participants.

All activities in this chapter involve the whole group working together. This adds to the participants' enjoyment of the games. Sometimes at the end of a long games session participants feel tired. Using the parachute during the last 15 to 20 minutes of a session is invaluable as it revitalises participants until the session ends.

Ball Flick

● EQUIPMENT

A parachute, one football or volleyball.

● GAME

Arrange the participants around the outside of the parachute. Instruct them to grip the edge using both hands and hold it at knee height. A football or volleyball is placed in the centre of the parachute. Call out 'One, two, three, up!' On the 'up' command the participants lift the parachute quickly by raising their arms. When their arms are above their head the parachute should rise upwards. When the parachute gets near its maximum height, participants should pull it down as fast as they can. This should flick the ball into the air as shown in figure 5.1. They should have five to six attempts, seeing how high the ball can be flicked into the air.

Figure 5.1

Safety Tips

▶ This game can only be played inside a sport hall with a high roof or outdoors.

ADVICE

- Advise participants to work together to get the timing of the upward and downward pulls right. This should send the ball further into the air.

VARIATIONS

- **Game variation:** Separate the participants into two teams. The teams should be standing around opposite sides of the parachute. Place the ball in the centre of the parachute and instruct the participants to try to shake the parachute so that the ball is thrown off their opponents' side. A point is scored each time the ball is shaken off the opponents' side. Play again until one team wins the game by scoring a set number of points, such as five.

Carousel  AGES 5-10

EQUIPMENT

A parachute.

GAME

Arrange the participants around the outside of the parachute. Instruct them to grip the edge using both hands and hold it at waist height. Participants begin walking round in a circle clockwise, turning the parachute as they go. Change speeds by telling them to move faster or slower. Call out a number of different commands for the participants to carry out. These include

- 'change'—participants move in the opposite direction (e.g., from clockwise to anti-clockwise);
- 'low'—participants move with the parachute held low;
- 'high'—participants move with the parachute held high;
- 'middle'—participants move with the parachute held at waist height;
- 'up and down'—participants alternate between holding the parachute high and low;
- 'in'—participants move toward the centre of the parachute so that the circle contracts;
- 'out'—participants stretch the parachute out again.

> ### Safety Tips
>
> ▸ Make sure participants do not stand too close to the person next to them to avoid tripping over each other.
>
> ▸ This activity should not be carried out if there are too many participants around the outside of the parachute, as they are likely to trip over each other.
>
> ▸ When calling 'in', ensure the participants do not move too close to the centre, otherwise they may trip on the parachute if it is trailing along the floor.

ADVICE

- Constantly change the commands to keep participants enthused.
- This can be used as part of a progressive warm-up. Start with slow movements, gradually increasing the intensity.

VARIATIONS

- **Easier/Harder:** Make up some of your own commands.
- **Harder:** Participants must carry out the opposite action to what has been called (similar to *Opposites,* see page 28).
- **Harder:** As the participants are moving, call out one of the colours found on the parachute. Participants holding on to that colour have to move under the parachute to a new position as quickly as possible (similar to *Colours,* see page 114).

Cat and Mouse  AGES 5-10

EQUIPMENT

A parachute.

GAME

This is a tag-type game that participants really enjoy playing. The set-up for this activity is shown in figure 5.2. Arrange approximately two-thirds of the participants around the outside of the parachute. Instruct them to grip the edge using both hands. Those holding the parachute should be kneeling. The remaining third become 'mice' and go under the parachute, except two who become 'cats' and go on top of the parachute. Both the

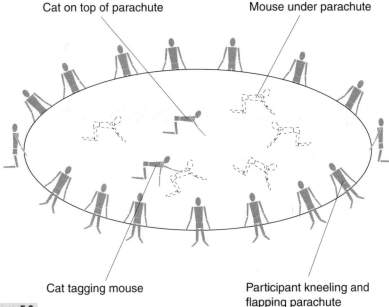

Cat on top of parachute

Mouse under parachute

Cat tagging mouse

Participant kneeling and flapping parachute

Figure 5.2

cats and mice should position themselves on their hands and knees. Instruct the participants around the edge to start flapping the parachute by moving it approximately 15 cm upwards and downwards.

After they have been flapping for a few seconds, start the game by shouting 'Go!' The cats crawl around on top of the parachute trying to tag the mice. If a mouse is tagged he or she must move out from underneath the parachute and help to flap. The game continues until all mice have been tagged, or for a set time (e.g., 1 to 2 minutes). Change the cats and mice with participants from the outside, then start the fun again.

Safety Tips

▸ Warn mice to be careful of collisions.

▸ Ensure cats do not tag too hard.

▸ Ensure cats stay on their hands and knees.

ADVICE

- Encourage honesty so that mice move straight out when they have been tagged.
- Tell the cats to work together to trap the mice if they are not tagging many.

VARIATIONS

- **Game variation:** Mice who have been tagged swap with one of the participants from the outside. Count how many mice are tagged in a set time, such as 1 to 2 minutes.

Colours  AGES 5-10

EQUIPMENT

A parachute.

GAME

Arrange the participants around the outside of the parachute. Instruct them to grip the edge using both hands, and keep both hands on one colour of the parachute. Call out '3, 2, 1, up!' and participants lift up the parachute above their heads. Then call out one of the colours. All those holding on to that colour should run under the parachute, aiming to appear through a space left by one of the other runners at the opposite side. After a few seconds call out 'Down!' Those still holding the parachute lower the parachute to the floor as quickly as possible. The runners try to get through to the other side and out before the parachute is lowered to the ground, otherwise they will be trapped underneath. Allow the runners out from under the parachute, then start again. Continue until all the colours have been called out two to five times.

> ### Safety Tips
>
> ▸ Warn the runners to be careful of collisions when moving under the parachute.
>
> ▸ Runners should be ready to crouch when the parachute is lowered to the floor.
>
> ▸ This should not be carried out if there are too many participants on each colour, as there will be too many runners going underneath at the same time.

ADVICE

- Vary the amount of time you allow runners to get across to the other side. Sometimes let them all across, other times trap them all.

● VARIATIONS

- **Game variation:** Instead of the participants lifting the parachute up and holding it above their heads, they could shake the parachute. Shout out the colour and those holding that colour crawl underneath the parachute to the other side.
- **Harder:** Any participants trapped underneath get the 'cooler' treatment (see *The Cooler,* page 117).

Dome ●●●●●●●●●●●●●●●●●●●●●●●●●●●●●● AGES 5-10

● EQUIPMENT

A parachute.

● GAME

This is an activity that requires the group to work together to form a dome using themselves and the parachute. Arrange the participants around the outside of the parachute. Instruct them to grip the edge using both hands and hold it at waist height. Call out '3, 2, 1, up!' and participants lift the parachute above their heads. Then call out 'Dome!' At this point participants should all step under the parachute, then bring the edge they are holding back over their heads and sit on the edge. This should make a dome shape (as shown in figure 5.3).

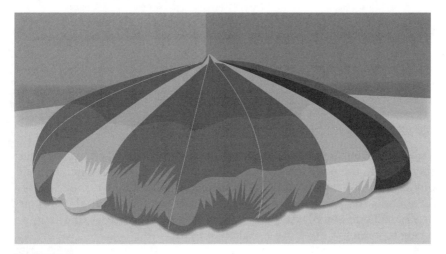

Figure 5.3

> ### Safety Tips
>
> ▶ Ensure participants all move quickly underneath when making the dome shape to avoid trapping participants' bodies with the parachute.

ADVICE

- Practise lifting the parachute in a few times before trying to sit inside.
- Ask the participants to sit on the material quickly to trap the air inside the parachute. The dome will stay up for approximately 30 seconds depending on the size of the parachute and whether the air can escape easily.

VARIATIONS

- **Game variation:** Ask a pair of participants from opposite sides of the parachute to change places once the dome is made.
- **Game variation:** Once the dome is made, instruct the participants to shuffle in towards the centre of the dome. This will cause the parachute to rise, much to the excitement of the children. Once everyone is near the middle, you can shake the parachute. This is always guaranteed to get a scream from all the participants, especially the younger ones.

Kites AGES 5-10

EQUIPMENT

A parachute.

GAME

Arrange the participants around the outside of the parachute. Instruct them to grip the edge using both hands and hold it at waist height. Call out '3, 2, 1, up!' and participants lift the parachute above their heads. As soon as the participants have their arms stretched out above their heads, call out 'Let go!' At this point participants release the parachute, trying to launch it high into the air, like a kite.

Safety Tips

▶ Only perform this activity outdoors or in high-roofed sport halls, where the parachute will not get caught in the roof.

▶ Do not play this game when the wind is blowing strongly, it just won't lift or the parachute will blow away.

ADVICE

• It is easy to spot participants who deliberately hold onto the parachute as it falls on their heads!

VARIATIONS

• **Game variation:** Separate the participants into two teams. Each team takes a few turns to perform the activity, with the winning team being the one that gets the parachute to fly furthest into the air.

The Cooler   AGES 5-10

EQUIPMENT

A parachute.

GAME

This activity is best played on a hot sunny day or at the end of a hard session. The set-up is shown in figure 5.4. Arrange half of the participants around the outside of the parachute. Instruct them to grip the edge using both hands and hold it at waist height. The remaining participants should lie down on their backs underneath the parachute. Those on the outside start flapping the parachute by moving it approximately 30 cm upwards and downwards. This causes a current of air to blow over those lying under it, thus cooling them. To finish, those on the outside shake the parachute over the faces of those under it. After approximately 1 minute, swap positions and start the fun again.

Figure 5.4

Safety Tips

▶ This game should not be carried out on cold days, especially if participants are wet as it can get quite chilly lying under the parachute.

ADVICE

- Advise the participants under the parachute not to sit up and to lie close together underneath the parachute.

VARIATIONS

- **Small groups:** Have fewer participants under the parachute with smaller groups (i.e., fewer than 12 in the group).

Rugby
Games

The activities in this chapter relate to rugby. The activities include a mix of warm-up ideas, technical practices and conditioned games. A number of activities involve support play and passing as these are two of the most important skills a rugby player needs. The conditioned games involve attacking and defending tactics, and participants will improve these skills with regular practice. The activities are suitable for playing rugby union or rugby league (except for *Ruck, Maul or Pass* on page 139, which is only applicable for rugby union), but use the correct tackling laws for your specific code.

Rugby uses revised rules to make the game more enjoyable for younger children. 'Touch' and 'tag' rugby are modified, non-contact versions of the game. In both versions tackling does not involve holding an opponent or trying to get them onto the ground. This reduces the risk of injury.

The Rugby Football Union (RFU) recommends that participants under eight years old should play 'mini-tag' rugby. Mini-tag rugby requires participants to wear a belt around their waist. The belt has two 'tags' attached by Velcro. If a participant is running with the rugby ball, opponents can 'tackle' them by removing a tag from their belt. In touch rugby a 'tackle' is made when a defender touches the ballcarrier with both hands on their hips. The touch should be on the side of the ballcarrier's body. In both mini-tag rugby and touch rugby, once the ballcarrier is tackled, they must stop and pass the rugby ball to a team-mate. After a specified number of tackles, the team in possession loses the rugby ball to their opponents. Throughout this chapter tackling is referred to as touch or tag tackling.

If you have enough tag belts, use them wherever possible. If you do not have enough to go around the group, then use 'touch tackles'. It is possible to use all the activities with full-contact tackling, but only after you have taught participants the correct techniques for tackling and falling safely. If you are unsure how to teach rugby progressions, gain relevant rugby coaching qualifications before using full-contact tackling.

No games include kicking skills. This is because the activities concentrate on improving participants' passing techniques and support play. After these skills have been learnt, you can then teach effective kicking skills, passing techniques and support play. Should you wish to incorporate kicking into your sessions, *Draw and Pass* and *Numbers Attack* (pages 129 and 135) are two games which can be adapted. Some activities can also be adapted for use in other specific sports. See the Variations section of each activity for further information.

It is important to understand the key rugby terms used in the chapter. If required, you can find more information on the International Rugby Board website (www.irb.com) in the *Laws and Regulations* section.

- **Dummy pass:** A player in possession of a rugby ball fakes a pass to a team-mate. The player pretends to pass the rugby ball, but keeps hold of it at the usual point of release.

- **Forward pass:** When in possession of the rugby ball a player cannot pass to a team-mate who is standing nearer the opponents' goal line. This is a mistake made frequently by participants new to rugby. Some of the games included here allow passes to be made in any direction because they should be used as part of a warm-up or to develop passing techniques. The games that involve passing skills and players attacking a goal line require the players to pass the rugby ball backwards as stipulated by the laws of the game.

- **Goal line, try (and in-goal area):** On a rugby pitch there is an 'in-goal' area at either end. The lines that separate the field of play and the in-goal areas are called the 'goal lines'. Teams defend one in-goal area and attack the other one when in possession of the rugby ball. Teams score a try by 'grounding' the rugby ball on the ground in the opponent's in-goal area. The rugby ball must be held in the hand(s) or arm(s) when the scorer brings the rugby ball into contact with the ground. Alternatively, a team can score a try if the rugby ball is already on the ground in the in-goal area. In this instance the try scorer needs to put downward pressure on the rugby ball with his or her arm(s), hand(s) or upper body. It is possible to create goal areas in the activities if needed. The term 'goal line' is used throughout the chapter, and attackers score tries by grounding the rugby ball on or over this line.

- **Knock-on:** This often occurs when a player attempts to receive a pass from a team-mate. If the rugby ball is dropped and travels toward the opponents' goal line, it is said to be 'knocked on'. The rugby ball must touch an opponent or the ground as a player loses possession to be classified as a knock-on.

- **Maul:** A maul is a phase of play that consists of at least three players. It occurs when a player carrying the rugby ball is held by one or more opponents and one or more of the ballcarrier's team-mates bind to the ballcarrier. All players in a maul must remain on their feet and be moving towards a goal line. An example of this is when a player is held up in the tackle. One or two team-mates may assist by grabbing the ballcarrier's shirt and pushing him or her towards the goal line. The maul starts when the team-mates have bound to the ballcarrier.

- **Ruck:** A ruck is a phase of play where one or more players from opposing teams are contesting a rugby ball on the ground. This often occurs when a player is tackled and put onto the ground. This player must then promptly release the rugby ball. If players are competing for the rugby ball, they usually grab hold of each other, trying to push their opponents out of the way. When this happens, it is called a ruck.

- **Rucking:** Players contesting the rugby ball in a ruck are said to be 'rucking'. These players must stay on their feet and cannot go down on their knees.

- **Tackle:** Throughout the chapter tackling is referred as a touch or tag tackle. You can incorporate full-contact tackling in activities that include touch or tag tackles. You must be suitably qualified to teach full-contact tackling, and participants must have been successfully taken though the teaching progressions for tackling first.

Attacking Run

EQUIPMENT

Cones, four rugby balls per five participants.

GAME

This activity develops attacking skills when in possession of the rugby ball. It can also be applied to successful defending skills. Arrange the participants into groups of 15. Set up each group as shown in figure 6.1. Cone out a large working area for each group. Split each area into five segments called 'defensive zones'. Choose five defenders from each group. One defender stands in each of the zones. Instruct the defenders that

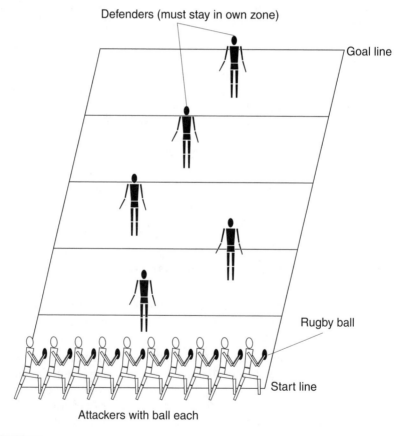

Figure 6.1

they can move anywhere they like inside their zone, but cannot leave it. The remaining participants start as attackers and line up on one of the end goal lines, each with a rugby ball. When the participants are set up, start the game by shouting 'Go!' On this command the attackers have to run to the opposite side of the area, getting past all the defenders to score a try. They have to get there without being tackled by any of the defenders. Any attackers who are tackled switch with the defender for the next round. Play for a set time, counting up the amount of tries scored by each participant. The player who has scored the most tries at the end of the time wins the game.

Safety Tips

▶ Use tag or touch rules for tackling (see chapter introduction). Full-contact tackling should only be incorporated when participants have been taught the correct techniques.

▶ Warn participants to be careful of collisions.

▶ Allow recovery periods in between rounds.

ADVICE

- Runners should try to dodge, side-step, swerve and change pace to get past the defenders.
- Runners should carry the rugby ball in both hands.

VARIATIONS

- **Game variation:** Attackers have half the number of rugby balls. They work with a partner to get one rugby ball through to the other side of their area. This means attackers can pass the rugby ball to their partner if they are about to be tackled.
- **Harder:** Play with full-contact tackling allowed.
- **Harder:** Separate each group into three teams. Teams should be identified by different-coloured bibs. One team defends, while the other two attack. The attackers attempt to run through each zone to score a try in order to earn a point. Any of the attackers who get tackled do not score and have their rugby ball removed. This means they have to act as supporting players and help to get the ball through the next time their team-mates run through the area. Continue until all the rugby balls have been removed, then change the defenders.

- **Small groups:** With smaller groups, attackers run one at a time and see how far they can get without being tackled.
- **Sport-specific:** This game can be adapted for use in other specific sports. For example, soccer players can dribble a ball through the area, while defenders attempt to tackle them.

Catch Tag

● EQUIPMENT

Cones, one rugby ball per four participants.

● GAME

Use this activity to develop passing and dodging skills. Arrange the participants into groups of four. Cone out an area approximately 10 m^2 for each group (see figure 6.2). Each group should nominate one runner

Rugby ball

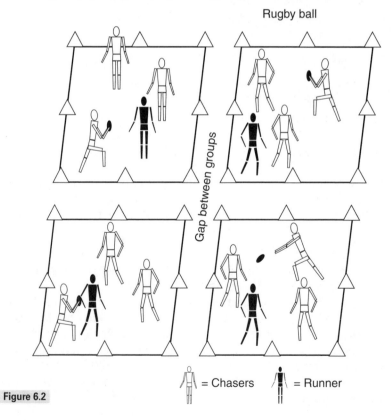

= Chasers   = Runner

Figure 6.2

and three chasers, then give one of the chasers a rugby ball. As soon as the game begins, all the participants must stay inside their area. The runner moves around avoiding the chasers. The chasers try to tag the runner with the rugby ball by touching him or her with it. The rugby ball must be in a chaser's hand to tag the runner and cannot be thrown at them. The chasers are not allowed to move if they have possession of the rugby ball. They can move if they do not have the rugby ball, so they should support their team-mates by moving next to the runner. A tag only counts if the runner is touched on the back or arms with the ball. It should not be pushed into the front of their body, at their head or in their face. Continue until the runner has been tagged or for a set time, such as 1 minute. Change the runner then start the game again.

Safety Tips

▶ Leave a 2-metre gap between each group's area. This should reduce the risk of dropped rugby balls rolling into another group's area.

▶ Warn participants to be careful of collisions.

▶ Ensure chasers do not tag too hard with the rugby ball.

▶ Ensure the chasers do not throw the rugby ball to make a tag. The rugby ball must be in a chaser's hand to touch the runner.

ADVICE

- Once the participants have grasped the game, you may notice that they use different types of passing techniques. Encourage them to use correct rugby passing techniques, such as the lateral pass.

- Change the number of chasers to make the game suitably challenging, depending on the ability of the players. Having more chasers usually makes it easier to tag the runner.

- With younger or less experienced participants, allow the chasers two steps when they have possession of the ball. This should make it easier for them to tag the runner.

VARIATIONS

- **Game variation:** Participants work in groups of 16, and the areas they are working in are joined by a channel (see figure 6.3). Chasers should wear bibs to identify themselves. Runners and chasers are allowed to move to a different area, but they must move through

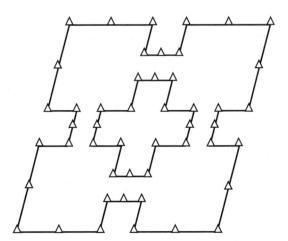

Figure 6.3

the connecting channel to get there. Chasers can tag any of the runners. Continue until all the chasers are caught, or for a set time (e.g., 1 minute).

- **Game variation:** Play a team game in one large area. One team starts as runners whereas the other team begins as chasers. The chasers work in pairs with one rugby ball per pair. The pairs try to tag as many runners as possible in a minute. If runners are tagged, they continue in the game but try to avoid being tagged again. Count how many times the runners are tagged, then swap the teams over so that the runners become chasers and vice versa. After both teams have had a chance to chase, the winning team is the one that has tagged the most opponents.

- **Game variation:** Play one game involving all of the participants inside a large area. Four participants begin as chasers, while the rest are runners. The chasers are given a bib each and are separated into pairs. Each pair should have a rugby ball. If a pair of chasers tag a runner, this person puts a bib on then joins the pair who tagged him or her. If a group of three chasers tags a runner, the runner becomes a chaser, but the four separate into pairs. One pair will need to collect a rugby ball before they rejoin the game.

Don't Let Them Drop AGES **8-16**

 EQUIPMENT

One rugby ball between two.

● *GAME*

This activity develops passing and receiving skills. Arrange the participants into groups of four. Each group makes a T-shape as shown in figure 6.4. Participants are numbered one to four with numbers one and four starting with a rugby ball. The participant in the centre (number two) is the 'focus player' as they are working more intensely than the others. The participants pass the rugby ball in the following sequence:

- Number four passes to number two.
- Two passes the rugby ball back to four.
- One passes to two.
- Two passes to three.
- (Repeat of first move.) Four passes to two.
- (Repeat of second move.) Two passes back to four.
- Three passes to two.
- Two passes to one.

Participants make eight passes, with participant number two making four out of the eight passes. The sequence can be repeated for a set time (e.g., 1 to 2 minutes) or until a rugby ball has been dropped. Participants rotate positions and continue the activity until each of them has been the focus player.

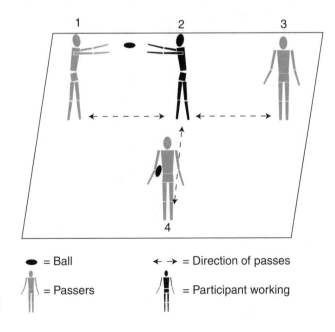

Figure 6.4

Safety Tips

▶ Instruct participants to use communication skills to avoid those receiving a pass being hit by the ball.

▶ All passes should be aimed at the centre of the body. This should reduce the risk of receivers being hit in the face by balls passed to them.

ADVICE

• Advise participants to pass slowly until they are familiar with the passing sequence.

• Advise participants to give a target with their hands indicating where they want the pass to be given.

VARIATIONS

• **Harder:** Instruct participants that they do not have to pass in sequence. Those on the outside of the focus player should vary the order in which they pass the ball to him or her. Again participants must communicate in order to avoid two passes being given at the same time.

• **Large groups:** This game can be adapted for groups of five (see figure 6.5) or groups of six (see figure 6.6). There are two focus players and three rugby balls needed in this second version.

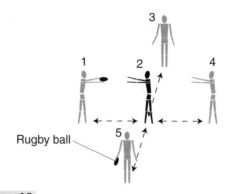

Figure 6.5

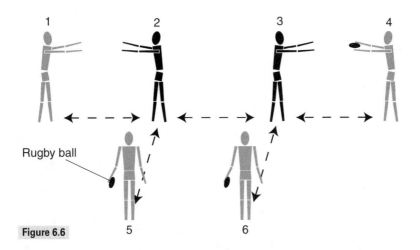

Rugby ball

Figure 6.6

Draw and Pass

AGES **8-16**

EQUIPMENT

Cones, one rugby ball per three participants.

GAME

This activity develops passing and receiving skills. It is very good for working on the timing of a pass in a situation where one defender faces two attackers. Arrange the participants into groups of nine. For each group, cone out a channel approximately 10 m × 20 m. In each channel participants work in smaller groups of three. In each of these groups there should be two attackers and one defender. They line up on the side of the channel (as shown in figure 6.7) and one of the attackers in each group has a rugby ball. When they are set up, start the game by shouting 'Go!' On this command the first group begins. The two attackers try to score a try, going against the defender. The attackers run down the side of the channel then into it around the last cone on that side. The defender runs in the opposite direction and into the channel by crossing the goal line. Once in the channel, the attacker with the ball tries to sprint past the defender or 'draw and pass'. This means they attract the defender to them then pass to the support player, who should have a clear run to the goal line.

Defenders can stop a try being scored by tackling the ballcarrier or forcing the ballcarrier out of the channel. Any try is disallowed if the attackers break one of the laws of the game (e.g., make a forward pass or knock the ball on). Once the attack has finished, one of the attackers switches roles with the defender then joins the back of the relevant line.

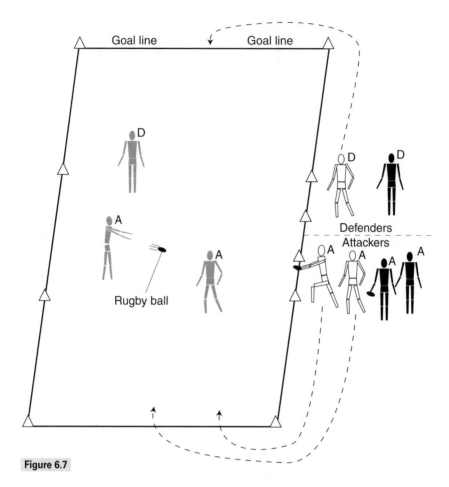

Figure 6.7

After these three participants have moved out of the channel, the next three can begin. Continue until all participants have had five turns as the defender.

Safety Tips

▶ Use tag or touch rules for tackling (see chapter introduction). Full-contact tackling should only be incorporated when participants have been taught the correct techniques.

▶ Warn participants to be careful of collisions.

▶ Ensure the participants waiting in the lines are a few metres away from the edge of the channel.

⬤ *ADVICE*

- There are a number of technical aspects that could be mentioned to the participants, as follows. The ballcarrier should
  - run fast,
  - draw the defender before passing,
  - keep checking to see where their supporting team-mate is,
  - use dummy passes to deceive the defender,
  - pass backwards if giving the ball to their partner.
- The support player should
  - stay slightly behind the ballcarrier,
  - not run too close or too far away from the ballcarrier,
  - give a target with their hands to show where they want to receive the pass.

⬤ *VARIATIONS*

- **Game variation:** Set up a series of adjacent channels (see figure 6.8). Participants move from one channel to the next, with the attackers trying to score at opposite ends of adjacent channels. After the last channel they should return to the start, then switch with the defender.

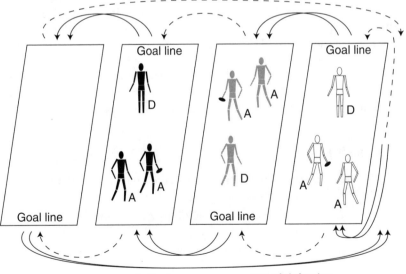

——→ = run of attacker   − − −▸ = run of defender

Figure 6.8

- **Game variation:** Allow participants to kick the rugby ball when attempting to beat opponents.
- **Harder:** With more experienced participants, play with two attackers and two defenders.
- **Harder:** Delay the defenders' start but get them to go into the channel from the side to vary the angle they are running at the ballcarrier. The attackers have to work out new strategies of scoring against the defender.
- **Harder:** Allow full-contact tackling.

How Fast Can You Pass? AGES 5-10

EQUIPMENT

One rugby ball per six to eight participants.

GAME

Use this activity to develop passing skills. Arrange the participants into groups of six to eight and give each group a rugby ball. Participants stand in a circle, facing the centre, with a gap of approximately 5 m between each of them. One of the participants is made the 'runner' and competes against the rest of the group in a race. The runner starts by passing the ball to the person standing to their left, then sprinting round the outside of the circle. The remaining participants must pass the ball around the circle. Each of them should receive a pass then move the ball to the person standing next to them. The runner wins the race if they get back to their starting position before the ball is passed to the first catcher, and vice versa. The next participant in the circle now has the ball and becomes the runner, starting the next race off in the same way.

Safety Tips

▶ Ensure the runner keeps an eye on the ball as they get back to their gap.

▶ Only play on wet grass if all of the participants have suitable footwear (i.e., rugby or football boots). If played on other surfaces, ensure the ground is not slippery.

ADVICE

- Repeat the activity but with the runner and rugby ball going the other way round the circle. This means passers work on sending the rugby ball in both directions.
- Vary the size of the circle depending on age and ability.
- If any of the passers drop the rugby ball, the runner wins the race.

VARIATIONS

- **Game variation:** Passers have to throw the ball around the circle twice, while the runner must also complete two laps.
- **Game variation:** Different groups can compete against each other. Everyone in each group must take a turn as the runner, with the team that finishes first winning the contest.
- **Game variation:** Passers must perform a skill (e.g., move a rugby ball around the waist) before passing the ball, while the runner has to complete two laps.
- **Striking/fielding/invasion games:** This game can be adapted for use in other passing/receiving and throwing/catching activities using the same rules, like cricket, basketball or netball.

Keep Away
AGES **5-16**

EQUIPMENT

Cones, one rugby ball per four to five participants.

GAMES

Use this activity to develop passing and receiving skills. Arrange the participants into groups of four or five. Cone out an area approximately 7 m² for each group. Participants must stay inside the area they are working in. Each group nominates one 'defender'. The remaining participants are 'passers', one of them being given a rugby ball. The passers are not allowed to move when they are in possession of the ball and try to make 10 passes. The defender tries to intercept passes or tackle the ballcarrier before the passers can make all 10 passes. At the end of each game change the defender and start the game again. The passers succeed if they make the 10 passes without dropping the ball. The defender succeeds if they tackle an opponent when they have possession or intercept a pass. The defender also succeeds if one of the passers drops the rugby ball, moves when he or she has possession of the ball or receives a pass outside his or her coned area.

Safety Tips

▶ Use tag or touch rules for tackling (see chapter introduction). Full-contact tackling should only be incorporated when participants have been taught the correct techniques.

▶ Warn participants to be careful of collisions.

▶ Leave at least a 2-metre gap between each group's area. This should reduce the risk of dropped rugby balls rolling into another group's area.

ADVICE

- Ensure all the passers in each group make a contribution by insisting they all touch the rugby ball a specific number of times (e.g., passers must make at least two passes each).
- The defender should not be in very long, so instruct them to work hard to close the passers down when they have possession. This should make the game more realistic.
- Instruct the passers to use dummies to deceive the defender.
- Advise the passers to draw the defender to them before passing to give more time to the receiver.

VARIATIONS

- **Easier/Harder:** Modify the size of the area.
- **Easier/Harder:** Change the numbers of passers and defenders (e.g., four versus two, two versus one, two versus two).
- **Game variation:** After a specified number of passes, the passers must attempt to score a try by touching the ball down on a specified side of the area.
- **Harder:** To make it more difficult for the passers, allow only certain types of passes (e.g., no passes above head height).
- **Harder:** Arrange the participants into groups of 15 and then separate them into three teams of five. Teams should be identified by using different-coloured bibs. Cone out an area for each group (approxi-

mately 20 m^2). The activity is still played as a possession game, except one team begins by defending, while the other two teams try to make the set number of passes. The two teams of passers can work together to make the allocated number. If one participant makes a mistake (such as dropping the ball), all in his or her team now become the defenders. Again the other two teams work together to make the set number of passes. Points are awarded to both teams if the passes are completed. One team then plays in defence. If the passing teams are successful, one of them changes roles with the defenders. Play for a set time, with the team scoring the most points at the end being declared the winner.

- **Small groups:** With smaller groups this activity can be played with the whole group in one area. The ratio of defenders to passers should be approximately one to four.

Numbers Attack AGES **5-16**

EQUIPMENT

One bib (or tag belt), cone and rugby ball each.

GAME

Use this activity to develop attacking and defending skills. Arrange the participants into groups of 10, then separate each group into teams of five. Cone out a working area for each group approximately 20 × 30 m. (as shown in figure 6.9). One team in each group wears bibs. Number the players in each team one to five. Teams stand at opposite sides of the area and take turns to attack and defend. Place half of the rugby balls beside each team. The instructor calls out one of the numbers, and participants so numbered compete against each other. The player for the attacking team picks up a rugby ball and runs to the end of the area. Attackers enter the area by crossing their own goal line. Meanwhile their opposite number has run to the opposite end, again entering the area by crossing the defending team's goal line. The attacker attempts to run past the defender then score a try. The defender attempts to stop a score by tackling the attacker. After a try has been scored or a tackle made, both participants return to the starting position ready for you to call out the next number. Participants should be reminded which team is attacking and defending before each number is called. The game continues until one team has scored a set number of tries (e.g., 10) or for a set time (e.g., 5 minutes).

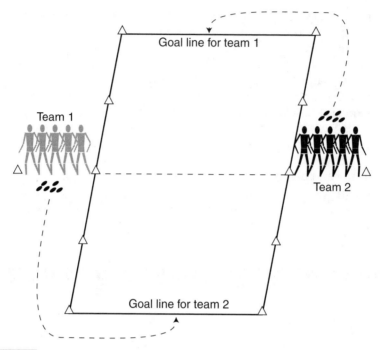

Goal line for team 1

Team 1

Team 2

Goal line for team 2

Figure 6.9

Safety Tips

▶ Use tag or touch rules for tackling (see chapter introduction). Full-contact tackling should only be incorporated when participants have been taught the correct techniques.

▶ Warn participants to be careful of collisions.

▶ Ensure the participants waiting in line are a few metres away from the edge their area.

✸ ADVICE

- Where appropriate, ensure that participants from opposing teams are numbered to match their ability.

- Change the numbering frequently so that participants can have a go against other opponents. Again, attempt to match up competitors by ability where possible.

- Vary the order the numbers are called in to keep the participants on their toes.

- This is a great activity to play towards the end of a session, as the participants and areas are organised for them to finish with a small-sided game.

VARIATIONS

- **Game variation:** Allow participants to kick the rugby ball when attempting to beat opponents.
- **Game variation:** Call more than one number, but only the first participant should pick up a rugby ball.
- **Game variation:** Throw a rugby ball into the middle of the area, then call out a number. Participants compete to get to the rugby ball first. Whichever participant does so becomes the attacker, while their opponent defends.
- **Harder:** Change the rules so that the defenders work in pairs taking turns to prevent their opponents scoring. Call out two to five numbers for the attackers.
- **Sport-specific:** This game can be adapted to other specific sports such as soccer. Set up goals in the middle of the goal lines. The attacker dribbles the soccer ball down the side of the area, then over the goal line. Attackers attempt to score in the opponent's goal but must cross the halfway line before shooting.

Removable Rugby  AGES 8-16

EQUIPMENT

One bib (or tag belt), cone and rugby ball each.

GAME

Use this activity to develop attacking and defending skills. Arrange the participants into groups of 12, then separate each group into teams of six. Each group should be set up as shown in figure 6.10. Cone out a large area for each group approximately 30 × 40 m. Teams stand on the shorter sides of the area at opposite ends, facing their opponents. One team wears bibs and defends their goal line while attacking the line the opposing team is standing on. A rugby ball is placed on the ground 5 m in front of each participant. Start the game by shouting 'Go!' All participants move into the area, pick up a ball then attempt to score a try by touching it down over the opposing goal line. Obviously, with no defenders,

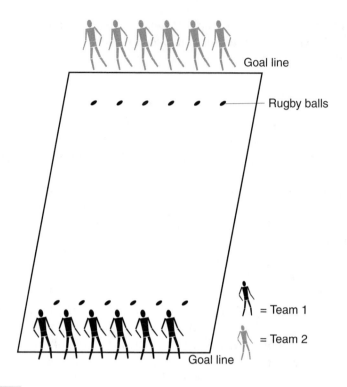

Goal line

Rugby balls

= Team 1

= Team 2

Goal line

Figure 6.10

all the participants should manage to do this. A point is scored for each try, which should mean six points per team.

Participants set up again but will be attacking in the opposite direction from the last round. The rugby balls are again placed on the ground, but this time remove one ball from each team. As all the participants cannot pick up a rugby ball, teams now have a decision to make. The spare participant can either defend, attempt to tackle opponents carrying a rugby ball or support their own players who do have one. Again a point is scored for each try, but this time if a participant is tackled, their ball is out of the game for that round. Once again line up the participants so that they are attacking the opposite goal line, then remove another rugby ball from each team. The game continues until all the balls have been removed. The team scoring the most points wins the game.

ADVICE

- Remember to keep score of how many tries each team has scored.

- Any rugby balls knocked on or passed forward are out of the game for the remainder of the round.

- Encourage the teams to decide on their tactics before each round.

VARIATIONS

- **Game variation:** Start with rugby balls placed randomly in the working area. Participants can pick up any one of them to score.

- **Harder:** Rugby balls are placed in front of participants from one of the teams, who begin as attackers. They continue for as many rounds as they can. Rugby balls are removed only if one has been dropped or if a tackle has been made. Thus if all the attackers are tackled in the first round, they have scored no tries and have all their rugby balls removed. However, if they all scored they will still have all the balls for the next round. The attackers continue until all the balls have been removed, then they switch places with the defenders. The team that attacks second tries to beat the score set by its opponents.

Ruck, Maul or Pass  AGES 11-16

EQUIPMENT

One cone and rugby ball per 10 participants.

● GAME

During rugby matches, changes in possession often occur when a player has been tackled. It is therefore essential that teams are organised so that they keep the rugby ball when one of them goes into contact. Use this activity to develop the team play and organisation needed to do this. It is a conditioned game which should only be used when instructing older or more experienced participants. The participants should know how to tackle correctly and how to fall safely after being tackled. It is also important that they have been taken through developmental work on rucks and mauls.

Arrange participants into groups of 10. Within each of these groups, separate the participants into teams of five. One team puts bibs on to identify themselves. Cone out an area approximately 40 × 15 m for each group. The shorter sides are the goal lines, with each team attacking the lines opposite them. The teams then play against each other, but the following conditions are made to the laws of the game. Participants should be informed that if a player in possession of the rugby ball is tackled or held, you will shout either 'ruck', 'maul' or 'pass'. The team must attempt to retain possession using whichever method is called. No kicking should be allowed and after a try is scored, the team conceding the try gets possession at the halfway line to start the game again. Play for a set time, such as 5 minutes, or until one team has scored a set number of tries (e.g., 5 to 10).

Safety Tips

▶ This activity should only be used if participants have been taught the correct techniques for tackling and falling after tackling. Participants must also have done the development work on rucks and mauls. If you are unsure of these, you should gain relevant rugby coaching qualifications before using this activity.

▶ Ensure you watch carefully for any infringements around the rucks and mauls. If you are unsure of these, you should gain relevant rugby coaching qualifications before using this activity.

● ADVICE

- The area should be quite narrow, as this should bring about more opportunities for tackles to be made.

- Ensure the participants run forwards, not sideways or backwards.

- Participants can practise the game first by playing without defenders. The teams should work across the pitch, listening for your commands. When you shout one out, the team acts as if it has opponents and carries out the required action.

● *VARIATIONS*

- **Game variation:** Only call out one command (e.g., 'ruck') for a set time to work on any weaknesses a team may have.

- **Game variation:** Turn the activity into a specific skills practice. Set up a channel (similar to the one in *Attacking Run,* page 122), which is divided into zones. Have two or three defenders in each zone. The remaining participants work in groups of five and are attackers. The attackers have one ball between each group and try to get through the channel. In each channel the ballcarrier must take the rugby ball into contact and then set up a ruck, maul or pass to a team-mate, depending on your call. Withdraw the calls to evaluate whether the participants are learning from their experiences.

Try AGES **5-16**

● *EQUIPMENT*

One cone and rugby ball between two participants.

● *GAME*

Use this activity as part of a progressive warm-up. Cone out a rectangular area, large enough to accommodate the whole group. The shorter sides are designated the goal lines for this activity. Arrange the participants into pairs, giving one participant from each pair a rugby ball. Participants run around the area passing the ball back and forth with their partner. If you shout the command 'try', the participant in possession of the rugby ball becomes the attacker. The attacker attempts to score a try by running to either of the goal lines and touching the rugby ball down on or over the line. Their partner becomes a defender and attempts to stop the attacker scoring by tackling them. A point is awarded to the participant who is successful. Pairs begin moving and passing again ready for the next call of 'try'. Play for a set time, such as 3 minutes. Within each pair, the winner at the end of this time is the one who has scored the most points.

Safety Tips

▸ Use tag or touch rules for tackling (see chapter introduction). Full-contact tackling should only be incorporated when participants have been taught the correct techniques.

▸ Warn participants to be careful of collisions.

▸ Ensure the area is large enough to accommodate the group.

ADVICE

- If used as part of a progressive warm-up, allow the participants to move around passing for a few minutes before calling 'try'.
- Participants should make quick passes and stay within 5 m of their partners when moving around the area.
- After 'try' has been called, the ballcarrier should dodge and use feints to avoid the defender.
- Instruct participants to pass the rugby ball using different methods (e.g., passing with two hands, one hand, or above the head). Or ask them to perform a skill (e.g., circling the ball around the waist) before passing to their partner.

VARIATIONS

- **Game variation:** Insist the attacker run past the defender to score.
- **Game variation:** Pairs work in their own smaller area.
- **Game variation:** Attackers can play for two points. In this version if the attacker scores at one goal line, they are also allowed to attack the other one.

Soccer
Games

The following activities relate to soccer, comprising a mixture of games, warm-up activities and skill practices. Collectively they can be used to develop passing, dribbling, heading and shooting skills, among others. Most of the activities are aimed at younger participants; however, some are suitable for older participants.

When you coach soccer, use the correct size of soccer ball for participants' age and ability. The English Football Association (FA) recommends that

- under-eights use a size three ball,
- under-elevens use a size four ball and
- over-elevens use a size five ball.

In this chapter participants with poor strength or low ability should use smaller soccer balls. If you use portable goals for the shooting game, they should be pinned or weighted to prevent them toppling forward. The goals should be sized correctly, according to the age and experience of the players. Participants should wear shin guards during activities involving tackling.

Admiral's Inspection   AGES 5-7

 EQUIPMENT

Cones, one soccer ball each.

 GAME

Use this activity to develop dribbling and shielding skills. Cone out an area large enough to accommodate the whole group. Participants should imagine they are in the Navy and are out at sea on a ship. Give each participant a soccer ball and instruct them to dribble their ball around the coned area. Participants should keep close control of their ball and stay inside the coned area. Various commands are given by you, each of them having a specific action or response that the participants must carry out.

These include

- 'tip to starboard'—Participants dribble their soccer ball to a nominated side of the coned area (to stop the ship from capsizing).
- 'tip to port'—Participants dribble their soccer ball to the opposite side of the coned area.
- 'pirate attack'—You try to steal the players' soccer balls and kick them out of the coned area. The participants whose soccer balls are kicked out are allowed back into the area after they have completed a skill (e.g., dribbling round the outside of the area).
- 'admiral's inspection'—Participants must stand to attention and salute the inspecting admiral (i.e., you).
- 'hoist the main sail'—Participants kick their soccer balls into the air then try to catch them before they bounce.
- 'mutiny'—Participants try to kick the other players' soccer balls out of the coned area. Participants who lose their balls have to try to get somebody else's and kick that out of the coned area.

Safety Tips

▶ Warn the participants to be careful of collisions.

▶ If 'hoist the main sail' is called, participants must not kick their soccer ball too high into the air.

▶ If 'mutiny' is called, participants attempting to steal a soccer ball from an opponent must be careful when they are making tackles.

ADVICE

- Add one new instruction at a time.
- Instruct participants how to salute correctly. If they get this wrong when the admiral makes his or her inspection, have them perform a fun challenge.
- Shielding and turns can be taught as the participants are playing the game.

VARIATIONS

- **Game variation:** Let one of the participants lead the game.
- **Invasion games:** This game can be adapted to other sports such as basketball. Participants dribble the basketball around the coned area following the same instructions, but adapting the responses to be more specific. For example, when 'hoist the main sail' is called, participants throw their ball into the air and clap as many times as they can before catching the ball again.

Doctor, Doctor   AGES 5-13

EQUIPMENT

Cones, one bib between two, one soccer ball each.

GAME

Use this activity to develop passing skills. The game is shown in figure 7.1. Arrange the participants into groups of 10, then separate each group into two teams of five, one of which wears bibs. Cone out two areas of 3 m². These should be positioned approximately 20 m apart and are called the 'surgeries'. There should be one surgery for each team. One participant from each team should be nominated to start as the 'doctor'. Doctors should stand in their respective surgeries. The remaining participants should be given a soccer ball. Start the game by shouting 'Go!' Participants with the soccer balls dribble up to an opponent and try to 'injure' them. To do this they pass the soccer ball at them, attempting to hit them below the knee. Participants can avoid being hit by dodging any shots aimed at them. Any participants who are hit (and therefore 'injured') are not allowed to move. They should kneel on the ground with their soccer ball under them. They can rejoin the game if they are tagged by their doctor, who must run out of their surgery to do this. If the doctor does leave the surgery, the opposing team can win the game by hitting him or her with the soccer ball. Again this should be below the knee. One round lasts until one of the doctors has been hit, when the opposing team scores a point. Continue the game until all of the participants have had a turn as the doctor. The winning team will be the one that has scored the most points at the end of the game.

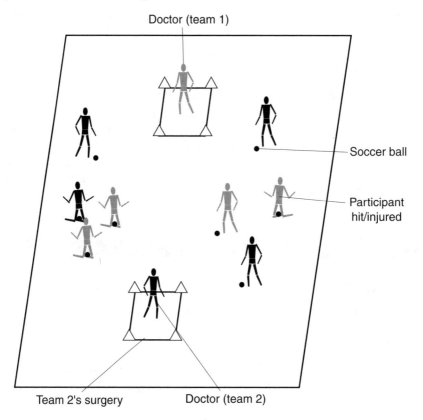

Figure 7.1

Safety Tips

▶ Warn participants to be careful of collisions.

▶ Watch carefully for players hitting the ball too hard or too high.

▶ Ensure the participants know why the ball must kept low and how to do this. They should do the following:

  • Keep their head over the soccer ball as they strike it and not lean back.

  • Use the inside of the foot to pass the ball.

  • Hit the ball just above its centre.

▶ Instruct participants to dribble close to opponents to pass the soccer ball at them.

ADVICE

• Inform the participants of the general tactics of the game. These should be to hit the outfield players first, then hit the doctor as they try to help their injured team-mates.

• Injured participants shout for help by calling 'Doctor, Doctor'.

• Make sure those participants who are hit stay where they are and do not move closer to the doctor.

• To help the attackers, instruct them to fake a pass to get their opponent to jump and then hit them as they land.

• Add the 'house call' rule. When you call out 'house call', the doctor must leave the surgery to help any injured participants. This helps speed up the game and allows those who are injured to be freed and join in the game again.

VARIATIONS

• **Game variation:** Play without a doctor and give all the participants a ball. If a player gets hit, any team-mates can tag them, enabling them to rejoin the game. A team wins if all the opponents are injured at the same time. If this does not happen in a set time (e.g., 3 minutes), count up the number of hits each team has scored to decide the winners.

• **Large groups:** It is possible to play with three teams. Use bibs to identify each team. Participants score points for their team by hitting either of the two other doctors.

Dodge the Pass

● EQUIPMENT

Cones, one soccer ball each.

● GAME

Use this activity to develop passing skills, including the accuracy and timing of a pass. Arrange the participants into groups of 10 to 12. For each group, cone out a rectangular area approximately 15 × 20 m. Each participant should place a soccer ball on one of the longer sides of their area. Two participants are chosen to be 'passers'. They should stand by the soccer balls, one on each side of the area. The remaining participants are 'runners' and stand on one of the shorter sides (see figure 7.2). When they are set up, start the game by shouting 'Go!' The runners attempt to cross to the opposite side of the area, avoiding soccer balls kicked at them

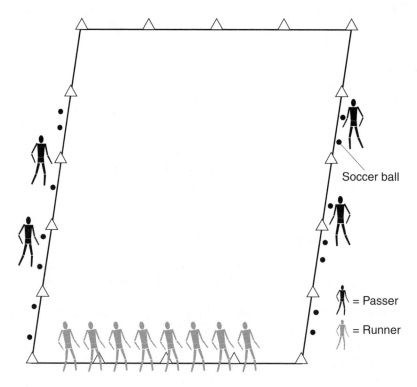

Figure 7.2

by the passers. The passers try to kick the soccer ball at the runners, aiming to hit them below the knee. They should not kick the soccer balls too hard and should go for accuracy rather than power. The passers can kick any of the soccer balls placed on their side of the coned area. Any runners hit become passers and move to the side of the area. The game continues until there is one runner left, who wins the game. The winner and the last person hit should become the passers for the next game.

Safety Tips

- ▶ Warn participants to be careful of collisions.
- ▶ Watch carefully for players hitting the ball too hard or too high.
- ▶ Ensure the participants know why the ball must kept low and how to do this. They should do the following:
  - • Keep their head over the soccer ball as they strike it and not lean back.
  - • Use the inside of the foot to pass the ball.
  - • Hit the ball just above its centre.

ADVICE

- • Runners should be given 10 seconds to get across to the other side of the coned area.
- • After each run, ask all the participants to collect the soccer balls and return them to the sides to speed up the game.

VARIATIONS

- • **Easier:** This game can be adapted when coaching young goalkeepers. They roll the ball underhand instead of kicking it to hit the runners.
- • **Game variation:** Play in teams. Participants in one team begin as passers while those in the other team start as runners. Runners continue going across the area even if they have been hit. Count up all of the hits in five rounds, then swap the teams' roles. Once each team has had a go at passing, the team scoring the most points wins the game.

Dribble Chase AGES **5-16**

 EQUIPMENT

Cones, one soccer ball between two.

GAME

Use this activity as part of a progressive warm-up. It can also be applied to develop dribbling and passing skills. Cone out an area large enough to accommodate the whole group. Arrange the participants into pairs and number them one and two. Number one starts as the 'chaser' and is given a soccer ball. When they are set up, start the game by shouting 'Go!' Number two moves around the coned area, trying to stay as far away from the chaser as possible. The chaser follows their partner dribbling the soccer ball, trying to stay as close to them as possible. Halt the game by shouting 'Stop!' At this point all participants should stop and stand still, with the chaser putting one foot on top of the soccer ball. Number twos turn around and face their partner. Chasers then pass the ball at their partners, attempting to hit them below the knee. A point is awarded if the chaser hits with the pass. Participants swap roles and repeat the game. Play for a set time (e.g., 3 minutes) or until one of the partners has scored a set number of points, such as five.

> **Safety Tips**
>
> ▶ Warn participants to be careful of collisions.
> ▶ Watch carefully for players hitting the ball too hard or too high.
> ▶ Ensure the participants know why the ball must kept low and how to do this. They should do the following:
>   • Keep their head over the soccer ball as they strike it and not lean back.
>   • Use the inside of the foot to pass the ball.
>   • Hit the ball just above its centre.

 ADVICE

- Watch carefully for participants moving after the stop command is given.
- Change the partners after each game to maintain motivation. Participants should start the new game with zero points.
- Instruct the participants to keep their own score.

- Reinforce the key factors of dribbling:
  - Keep looking up between touches.
  - Keep close control of the ball.
  - Use all parts of both feet to move the ball.

VARIATIONS

- **Easier:** Mark out a smaller coned area for each pair. With no other participants to avoid, dribblers should find it easier to move around.
- **Game variation:** Participants who dribble out of the area or hit somebody else's soccer ball are not allowed to move. They must take their shots from that position after the stop command is given. This ensures that participants have close control of the ball and keep their heads up between touches.
- **Game variation:** On the stop command, chasers attempt to pass the ball through the legs of their partners, who stand facing them with their legs apart.
- **Game variation:** All participants have a soccer ball. The chaser and their partner move in the area dribbling their soccer ball. On the stop command, the chaser must hit the opponent's ball to score a point.

 Dribble Gates AGES 5-13

EQUIPMENT

Cones, one soccer ball each.

GAME

This activity develops dribbling skills, including speed and control of the ball. It can be used as part of a progressive warm-up or as a developmental practice. For the set-up of this activity see figure 7.3. Cone out lots of 'gates', these being two cones placed 1 m apart. There should be approximately one gate per participant. Give the participants a soccer ball each and instruct them to dribble their ball through as many gates as they can in a minute. When they are set up, start the game by shouting 'Go!' Participants dribble around the area trying to dribble through all the gates. Ask the participants to keep score of how many they dribble through and ask them to call out their score each time they pass between the cones forming the gate. If they go through every gate, instruct them not to stop but to go back through some of the gates again.

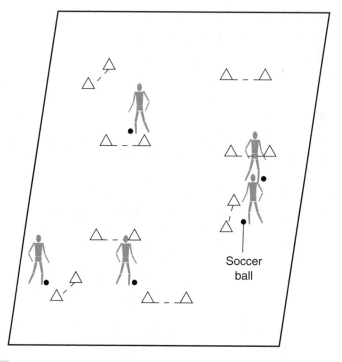

Soccer ball

Figure 7.3

✱ ADVICE

- With younger participants, use different-coloured cones for each gate so they are easily identified. For example, use two white cones for one gate, two green cones for another, and so on.
- Reinforce the key factors of dribbling:
  - Keep looking up between touches.
  - Keep close control of the ball.
  - Use all parts of both feet to move the ball.

⚫ *VARIATIONS*

- **Easier:** Participants work in pairs, one being a 'dribbler' while the other is a 'defender'. The defender attempts to slow the dribbler by getting to a gate first to prevent him or her moving through. If blocked, the dribbler must move to a different gate. This is a good variation if there are not enough soccer balls to have one each.
- **Easier/Harder:** Change the size of the area and the gates to change the difficulty.
- **Harder:** Participants are only allowed to use one foot to dribble the ball.
- **Harder:** Two defenders are chosen. The defenders attempt to steal the soccer balls from the other participants and kick them away (not too far though).

 **Dribble Pass** AGES **5-13**

⚫ *EQUIPMENT*

Cones, one soccer ball between two.

⚫ *GAME*

Use this activity to develop dribbling and passing skills. Arrange the participants into groups of 10, then separate each group into teams of five. Each team wears different-coloured bibs. Cone out a large working area of approximately 15 m² for each group. Teams stand on opposite sides of their area with each of the participants from one team having a soccer ball. These participants are called 'chasers'. When they are set up, start the game by shouting 'Go!' The participants from both teams move around staying inside the area. The chasers try to dribble their soccer ball close to an opponent and when they are within 5 m try to pass the soccer ball at them, aiming to hit them below the knee. They should not kick the soccer balls too hard and should go for accuracy rather than power. Their opponents try to avoid being hit by dodging out of the way of passes aimed at them. Instruct the chasers to keep score of how many times they hit an opponent. Total up the number of hits this team gets after a set time period, such as 3 minutes. The teams should swap roles and line up ready to start the game again. When both teams have had two turns chasing, the team scoring the most hits wins the game.

Safety Tips

▶ Warn participants to be careful of collisions.

▶ Watch carefully for players hitting the ball too hard or too high.

▶ Ensure the participants know why the ball must be kept low and how to do this. They should do the following:

  • Keep their head over the soccer ball as they strike it and not lean back.

  • Use the inside of the foot to pass the ball.

  • Hit the ball just above its centre.

▶ Instruct participants to dribble close to opponents to pass the soccer ball at them.

ADVICE

• Reinforce the key factors of dribbling to the chasers:
  • Keep looking up between touches.
  • Keep close control of the ball.
  • Use all parts of both feet to move the ball.
• To help the chasers, instruct them to fake a pass to get their opponent to jump, then hit them as they land.

VARIATIONS

• **Game variation:** Do not separate groups into teams but start with two chasers, the rest being 'runners'. Each time a runner is hit they collect a soccer ball and become a chaser. The game continues until there is one runner left, who wins the game. The winner and the last person hit should become the chasers for the next game.

Head Catch  AGES **5-10**

EQUIPMENT

One soccer ball per group.

GAME

This activity can help develop participants' confidence and skill in heading the ball. It is best played with small groups of fewer than 12 participants. Instruct the participants to make a circle around you, standing approximately 5 m away, and inform them of the rules. These are that you will face each one of them in turn and lob the ball gently underarm towards their heads. As soon as the ball has been released, you will shout either 'head' or 'catch'. The participant must do the opposite. So if you shout 'head', the participant should catch it. If 'catch' is called, the participant must head it back to you. The participants' aim is to carry out the correct action, scoring a point each time they do so. The activity continues for a set time (e.g., 3 to 5 minutes), with the participant scoring the most points at the end winning the game.

Safety Tips

▶ Ensure you have taught the participants how to head the ball correctly before playing this game.

▶ Ensure your throw is accurate. It should not be too low as this can sometimes strike the participant on the nose if they mis-time their header. Instruct them to keep their eyes open when they head the ball.

▶ Ensure the ball has no frays or pieces of leather hanging off it. If playing on a wet day, ensure all mud is cleaned off the ball before lobbing it to the participants.

ADVICE

- After working round the circle a few times, change direction and throw the ball to the same person twice to confuse the better players.
- Key coaching points for heading are to
  - keep eyes open,
  - use the forehead to head the ball,
  - lean back before heading and
  - follow through after contact.

VARIATIONS

- **Game variation:** Participants perform a fun challenge, like running round the circle backwards or saying a nursery rhyme, if they do the wrong action.

- **Game variation:** With older participants, get them to kneel if they perform the wrong action. They continue in the game, but if they make another mistake they sit down.

- **Game variation:** Older or more able participants can work in smaller groups or pairs with one of them throwing the ball and one heading. They must be able to throw the ball accurately to do this.

Rapid Fire   AGES 8-16

EQUIPMENT

Cones, one soccer ball each, one goal per 10 participants.

GAME

Use this activity to develop shooting, passing and goalkeeping skills. Arrange participants into groups of 10 and then separate each group into two teams of five. Teams should be numbered one and two and those in team one should wear bibs to identify themselves. Each group of 10 should be set up around a goal as shown in figure 7.4. Three participants from team one start as 'passers' and line up on the goal line 10 m to the right of the goalkeeper. The other two participants from team one begin as 'shooters', standing 5 m back from the edge of the 18-yard box. They should be positioned diagonally across the box from the passers. Team two is set up in a similar way. Again two participants begin as shooters and two as passers, but this time they are on the other side of the goal from team one. The remaining participant from team two starts as the goalkeeper. The passers from both teams need a soccer ball and the spares are placed beside them. The first passer from team one starts the game by passing the ball across the box for the first team one shooter to strike at goal. After the shot all the participants rotate positions. This occurs throughout the game in the following sequence.

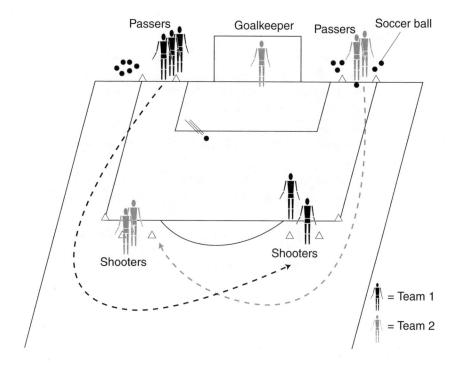

Figure 7.4

- Passer to shooter—the passer runs around the back of the opponents' shooters to their own shooting line.
- Shooter to goalkeeper—the participant who took the last shot goes into goal for the next shot from the opposing team.
- Goalkeeper to passer—after attempting to save a shot, the goalkeeper moves to his or her team's passing line.

If this sequence is followed correctly, the shooter should always be facing a shot from an opponent. Players in team one should shoot with the left foot throughout this round. Rounds should last for a set time (e.g., 3 minutes) and teams should switch lines at the end of each round. Keep score of how many goals are scored, and the team scoring the most after four to six rounds wins the game.

Safety Tips

▶ Ensure the passers' lines are not too close to the goal as inaccurate shots at goal may hit them. Participants must keep a careful watch on whomever is shooting in case the shot misses.

▶ Make sure participants running to the shooting position run around the outside of their opponents' shooting line.

▶ Ensure no loose balls roll in front of the goalkeeper. This should avoid the goalkeeper diving or tripping on them.

▶ The shot should not be taken too close to the goal. Ideally it should be struck from an area between the penalty spot and the edge of the 18-yard box.

ADVICE

• Ensure the pass is weighted correctly. It should almost have stopped as the shooter strikes at goal.

• When standing to the left of the goalkeeper, shooters should use their left foot to shoot and vice versa. Some participants will try to use their dominant leg on both sides. Try to ensure they practise shooting with both legs.

• Key coaching points of shooting include
    • go for accuracy before power (hit the target),
    • use the laces to strike the ball,
    • keep an eye on the ball,
    • take a high back-swing and follow through with the kicking leg,
    • lock the ankle of the kicking foot,
    • place the standing foot beside the ball and pointing toward the goal.

VARIATIONS

• **Game variation:** If you have goalkeepers, use them in goal instead of everyone having to take a turn in goal. Participants therefore move straight from shooter to passer.

- **Game variation:** Different scoring systems can be used to reward accuracy of shooting. For example, one point can be given for hitting the target, a bonus point can be given for a score and all a team's points lost if the ball flies over the bar.

- **Game variation:** Closer-range finishing can be practised, but insist the inside of the foot should be used to shoot.

- **Small groups:** With smaller groups participants can play individually, organised like one of the teams in the standard version. Play rounds, but ensure the participants change the order in which they go so that they are not shooting against the same opponent each time. Participants gain a point each time they score a goal, with the winner at the end being the person with the most points.

- **Small groups:** Another way of playing this activity individually is to start each participant on three points and three 'lives' while they are in goal. Participants try to avoid losing a point and thus a life for each goal that is scored past them. Goalkeepers stay in goal until they save a shot, or an opponent misses the goal. In this instance the shooter replaces the goalkeeper. When goalkeepers lose their last point, the player who knocked them out of the game becomes the goalkeeper.

 AGES **5-10**

 EQUIPMENT

Cones, one soccer ball each.

GAME

Use this activity to develop accuracy of passing as well as the correct weight of a pass. Arrange the participants into groups of 10 and then separate them into teams of five. Each group should be set up as shown in figure 7.5. Cone out an area approximately 15 × 35 m. Using more cones, separate each group's area into three zones lengthways. Teams stand in the end zones at opposite sides of the area. The zone between the teams is called 'no man's land'. This should be approximately 5 m wide and in the centre of the area. Give each participant a soccer ball and when they are set up, start the game by shouting 'Go!' Participants attempt to pass the ball into their opponents' zone. The aim of the game is to have as many balls as possible in the opposing team's zone when the game is stopped. Any balls that are kicked into a team's zone should be passed back across to their opponents' zone. Participants should aim to weight

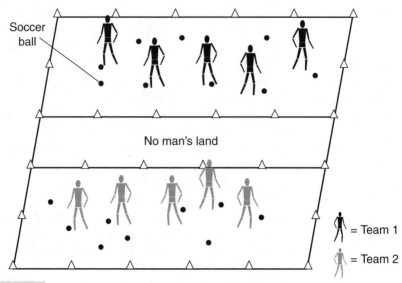

Soccer ball

No man's land

= Team 1

= Team 2

Figure 7.5

the pass correctly. Therefore, the soccer ball should not be kicked too gently as it will stop in no man's land nor too hard, otherwise it will go out the back of the opponents' zone. Balls that travel out of the opponents' zone are counted against the kicker's team. Play for a set time (e.g., 1 to 2 minutes) then end the game by shouting 'Stop!' Each team scores a point for every ball in the opposing team's zone and any ball kicked out the back of their own zone. The team with the most points wins the game.

Safety Tips

▷ Make sure the participants are aware of where the opposition is standing so that they do not kick the ball at them.

▷ Warn participants to be careful of collisions.

▷ Watch carefully for players hitting the ball too hard or too high.

▷ Ensure the participants know why the ball must be kept low and how to do this. They should do the following:

• Keep their head over the soccer ball as they strike it and not lean back.

• Use the inside of the foot to pass the ball.

• Hit the ball just above its centre.

● ADVICE

- Encourage honesty by ensuring participants do not pass any soccer balls after you have stopped the game.
- If possible have more soccer balls in each team's zone as a number of them will be kicked out the back and sides of the area.
- This game cannot be played on fast-rolling surfaces (e.g., in sport halls or on Astroturf).

● VARIATIONS

- **Easier:** One participant from each team stands at the back of the opposing team's zone and is allowed to kick any balls that have rolled out of the zone back into it.
- **Harder:** Participants are only allowed to pass the soccer ball with one foot.
- **Hockey:** This game can be adapted for use in hockey if playing on grass. Fast-rolling surfaces are not suitable as the hockey balls will usually roll out the back of the area.
- **Small groups:** Smaller groups can play against you.

Two Touch   AGES 8-16

● EQUIPMENT

Cones, one soccer ball per four participants.

● GAME

This is a great activity for developing good control and passing skills. The game uses the badminton scoring system, so some of the language used here is taken from that game. Arrange the participants into groups of four and cone out a 'court' for each one (see figure 7.6). Within each group, participants are separated into teams of two, and each team stands in one half of the court. The court is approximately 5 × 10 m, divided in the middle by a 'mini-goal'. The mini-goal is marked out using two cones and is approximately 1.5 m wide. One participant begins with the ball, becoming the 'server'. The server stands behind the 'baseline' on their side of the court and passes the ball through the mini-goal to the opponents' half to start a 'rally'. The serving team has one chance only to get the ball through. If the ball goes through the mini-goal, the players from the opposing team are allowed two touches to get it back through to their

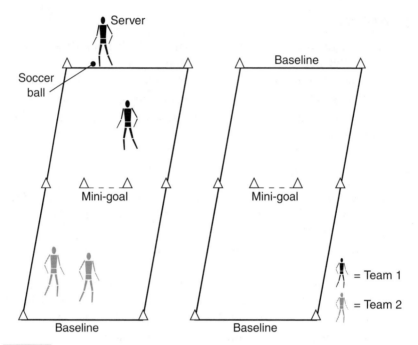

Figure 7.6

opponents. Team-mates must both take a touch, which means that one should control the ball and their partner should pass it back through the mini-goal. This continues until one team has won the rally.

A rally can be won if the following conditions are present:

1. A participant kicks a ball that is missed by an opponent and leaves the area crossing their baseline. The ball must roll over the baseline.

2. An opponent misses the mini-goal with the second touch.

3. Opponents do not get the ball back through the mini-goal in two touches. They cannot take fewer than or more than two touches. They must each have a touch of the ball, as mentioned earlier.

4. An opponent takes a shot that goes through the mini-goal but crosses out of the court down one of the sidelines.

5. A participant lets an opponent's shot go if it leaves the area over the baseline but does not roll along the floor, or if it rolls over the sideline.

Like in badminton, if a rally is won by the serving team, the servers score one point and the same server starts the next rally. The server continues to serve until his or her team has lost a rally. If the serving team loses the rally, the opposing team does not win a point as points can only be won by teams when they are serving. *This means when receiving service, a team tries to win a rally so that they have the opportunity to serve and therefore score points.* Just like in doubles play badminton when a team wins service back from their opponents, both players will have their chance to serve. This is except for the first 'innings' when only the first server gets to serve.

Safety Tips

▶ Watch carefully for players hitting the ball too hard or too high.

▶ Ensure the participants know why the ball must be kept low and how to do this. They should do the following:

- Keep their head over the soccer ball as they strike it and not lean back.
- Use the inside of the foot to pass the ball.
- Hit the ball just above its centre.

ADVICE

- Instruct the participants to try to win points using accuracy rather than power when passing.
- With younger or less able payers, make the goal bigger or allow more touches.
- Make the playing area size appropriate to the age and ability of the group.

VARIATIONS

- **Game variation:** Allow participants to play the ball back with one touch.
- **Game variation:** Play in groups of three using a slightly wider area and goal. Again participants should only play the ball back with two touches.
- **Game variation:** Play tennis rules for serving and scoring.

Tennis and
Badminton Games

The following activities relate to tennis, and some related to badminton. There is a mixture of skills practices, warm-up activities and games. Collectively the activities can be used to develop most tennis shots, footwork, decision making and tactical awareness.

Most activities can be played indoors using 'short tennis' equipment. For indoor sessions use plastic rackets and sponge balls when instructing younger participants. For outdoor sessions use rackets that are an appropriate size and weight for the participants. Provide younger or less able group members with rackets with smaller handles, if available, to give them more success. Younger or less able players should also use less bouncy tennis balls so that they have more time to get into position during the activities.

Most activities can be adapted easily for badminton and may not need modification. Some activities require modifications to make them suitable. If it is possible to adapt an activity to badminton, the information needed to do this is found in the Variations section.

In tennis or badminton sessions, often an instructor has more participants than can be accommodated because of the limited amount of court space. Thus a number of participants might have to sit out the action at any one time, waiting for their turn on court. Because children learn best when they are enjoying themselves, the activities found in this chapter aim to involve participants more frequently. Participants will not be off court for longer than a few minutes. With more involvement your group will enjoy the session more.

Catch to Score  AGES 8-16

EQUIPMENT

One racket, tennis ball and tennis court per six participants, chalk.

GAME

Use this activity to develop various tennis strokes. The aim is to improve the accuracy of these shots by hitting the tennis ball into different areas of the court. Arrange the participants into teams of six. Each team works on their own court and starts with one hitter, one server and four catchers. Split one side of each court into four equal areas, using the chalk. Number these areas one to four (as shown in figure 8.1). These will be target areas for the hitter to aim at.

Set up the activity as shown in figure 8.1. The catchers stand in a target area each. The hitter stands on the other side of the net to the catchers, at the back of the court. The server should stand on the same side as the hitter at the side of the court. Ideally they should have a number of tennis balls, but one will suffice. The server throws a tennis ball for the hitter to play a shot at. As the tennis ball travels, the server calls out the number of a target area. The hitter then tries to hit the tennis ball into that target area. If the hitter plays the tennis ball into the correct target area and it is caught by the catcher, the team scores a point. Rotate positions after 10 hits until every team member has been the hitter. The team scoring the most points at the end wins the game.

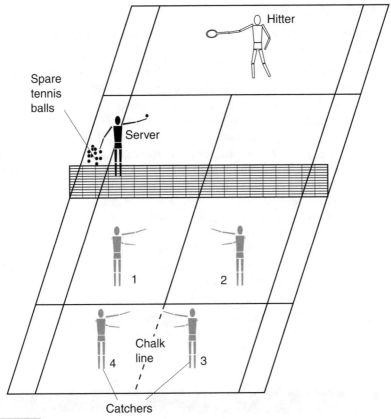

Hitter

Spare
tennis
balls

Server

1

2

Chalk
line

4

3

Catchers

Figure 8.1

ADVICE

- Make sure the server gives the call early enough.
- The server can feed the ball in different ways so that participants work on a number of different shots.
- Make sure the server throws the ball in the right place to get the hitter to work on the shot you have specified.

● *VARIATIONS*

- **Badminton:** This game can be played in badminton sessions using the same rules.

- **Game variation:** The hitter calls which target area he or she is aiming at, making the call before striking the ball.

- **Harder:** This variation is for advanced players. All the catchers have a racket and the team tries to keep a rally going. After the service, the hitter calls which area to aim at. If the shot is played into the right area, the catchers play the ball back to the hitter. The two closest to the net should play a volley shot, whereas the two at the back of the court should let the tennis ball bounce in the target area before returning it. The hitter should call out the number of the next target area with each return. The rally continues until the hitter plays a shot to the wrong area, or the catchers fail to return the tennis ball. The team should keep a record of how many shots were played in each rally. The team with the highest-scoring rally at the end of a set time period wins.

- **Small groups:** Play in groups of three with one server, one hitter and one catcher. The catcher starts in the middle of the court and moves to one of the target areas as the ball is served. The hitter attempts to hit the ball to the area where the catcher is now standing.

Champ of the Court — AGES **8-16**

● *EQUIPMENT*

One racket each, one tennis ball and tennis court per four to eight participants, chalk.

● *GAME*

Having more than four players per court can be a major problem with participants having to wait a long time for a game. *Champ of the Court* can accommodate more people per court and can be used to develop most tennis shots. Arrange the participants into groups of four, each group working on half a court. Use chalk to divide the court into two halves. One participant begins as the 'champ', with the rest beginning as 'challengers'. The challengers start on the opposite side of the net to the champ, lining up at the back of the court (see figure 8.2). The challengers' aim is to beat the champ, thereby replacing him or her. The first challenger steps onto the court and serves to the champ. They play the point out, then

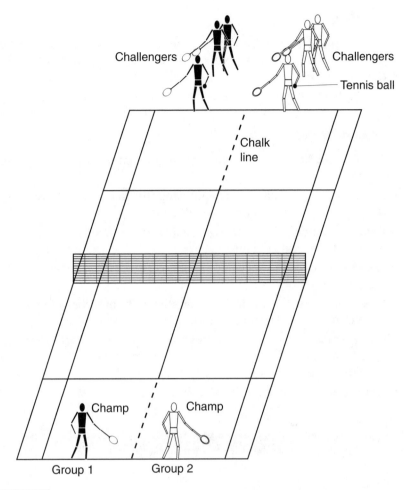

Figure 8.2

the challenger returns to the back of the line. The winner gains a point. Challengers take turns playing a point out against the champ. If one of them scores two points in a row, they replace the champ; if challengers win one point but lose the next rally, their score drops back to zero.

Safety Tips

▸ Make sure the participants who are waiting for their turn stand well back from the baseline.

✹ *ADVICE*

- Ask the players to shout out 'zero' or 'one' at the start of the rally depending on how many points they have won so that there are no arguments.
- All challengers start from zero if there is a change of champ.

✹ *VARIATIONS*

- **Badminton:** This game can be played in badminton sessions using the same rules.
- **Doubles:** Doubles can be played using the same rules. Obviously this should only be played on a full court.
- **Game variation:** The challenger has to score three or four points in a row to become champ.
- **Game variation:** Points can only be won by playing specific shots (e.g., a volley).
- **Game variation:** Start with a 'cooperative rally' of three or five shots to give the participants more practice.
- **Game variation:** Use conditioned areas of the court to develop specific shots. For example, use only the front half of the court to develop net play (similar to *Net Champ,* page 175).
- **Small groups:** Smaller groups can play on a full court.

Conveyor Belt   AGES 5-10

✹ *EQUIPMENT*

Cones, one racket each, one tennis ball per four participants.

✹ *GAME*

Use this activity as part of a progressive warm-up or as a competitive race. Each participant should be given a tennis racket, then they should be arranged into teams of four. Cone out starting and finishing lines approximately 20 m apart. Each team lines up at the start, with the front participants from each team balancing a tennis ball on their rackets. When they are set up, start the game by shouting 'Go!' Teams try to move the ball to the finishing line by passing it from racket to racket. The participant behind the person with the ball runs round in front of the ballcarrier before being passed the ball. Each time a participant passes the ball on they should move to the front of the line ready to receive the ball again. Thus the ball is passed along the rackets towards the finishing line. Teams try to get the tennis ball to the finishing line without dropping it onto the floor.

Safety Tips

▶ Warn participants to be careful of collisions.

▶ Participants should keep control of their rackets to avoid hitting others with it.

▶ Ensure there is a gap of approximately 5 m between each team.

ADVICE

- The ball can be passed further by spreading the participants out.
- Ensure participants are not using their hands to keep the tennis ball on the racket.

VARIATIONS

- **Badminton:** This game can be played in badminton sessions using the same rules.
- **Game variation:** Teams race against each other. The team crossing the finishing line first wins.
- **Game variation:** If the tennis ball is dropped onto the floor, the team must return to the start, then go again.
- **Game variation:** When participants are passed the tennis ball, they must pass the racket around their back before passing the ball on to the next team-mate.
- **Harder:** Participants hit the tennis ball into the air three times before they pass it on to the next person.

Learn the Lines AGES 5-13

EQUIPMENT

One tennis court per 10 participants.

🔹 *GAME*

Use this activity as part of a progressive warm-up and to help participants learn the names of the lines on a tennis court. Arrange the participants into groups of 10. Each group stands on a different tennis court. Instruct participants to spread out and find a space. There should be an equal number of participants on each side of the net. Shout out the name of a line on the tennis court, such as 'baseline' or 'centre service line'. Participants have to move to whichever line you have called and stand on it. For the names of the lines found on a tennis court, see figure 8.3.

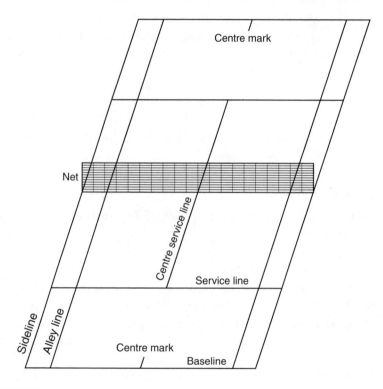

Figure 8.3

Safety Tips

▸ Ensure there are not too many participants on one court.

▸ Warn participants to be careful of collisions.

🔹 ADVICE

- If being used as part of a warm-up, make sure movements are progressive. For example, participants walk, then jog, then run to the lines as the warm-up develops.
- Add a fun challenge for the person who is last onto the line or makes a mistake, such as keeping the ball up five times or doing an animal impression.

🔹 VARIATIONS

- **Badminton:** This game can be played in badminton sessions using the same rules. For the names of the lines found on a badminton court, see figure 8.4. The game can also be adapted to other sports that use a marked court (e.g., basketball or netball).
- **Game variation:** Hop, sidestep or sprint to the lines instead of running.
- **Harder:** Ask questions instead of shouting a line. An example could be 'Which sideline is used in singles?'

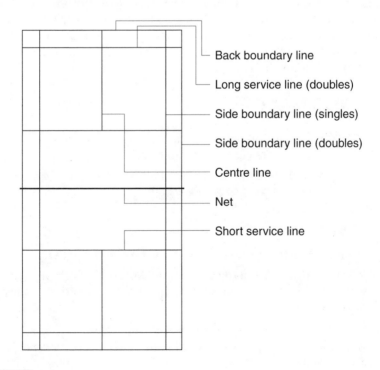

Back boundary line

Long service line (doubles)

Side boundary line (singles)

Side boundary line (doubles)

Centre line

Net

Short service line

Figure 8.4

- **Harder:** Provide the participants with a ball and racket each and get them to do coordination exercises, such as keeping the ball up on the forehand then backhand side of the racket or bouncing the ball on the ground with the racket, in between shouting out lines.
- **Small groups:** Use one court.

Line Rally

✹ EQUIPMENT

One tennis ball and racket each, one tennis court per 12 participants.

✹ GAME

Use this activity as part of a progressive warm-up. It should develop coordination and timing skills on the forehand and backhand. Each participant should have a tennis racket and tennis ball. Participants spread out around the courts and pick a line they will work at. They should be well spaced out, and should not work within 5 m of another participant. The aim is to hit the ball so that it lands on one side of the line, then the other. Participants try to keep this sequence going for as many shots as they can and should use one side of the racket then the other to play the ball back and forth.

> ### Safety Tips
>
> ▸ Don't have too many participants on one court (i.e., no more than 12 per court if possible).
> ▸ Warn participants to be careful of collisions, especially when retrieving stray tennis balls.

✹ ADVICE

- Demonstrate the correct grip before starting the activity.
- Inform participants of the correct footwork—a sidestepping action without crossing the feet, moving quickly into position to play the next shot.
- Instruct participants to hit the tennis balls gently.
- Watch for participants switching hands instead of playing backhand then forehand.

VARIATIONS

- **Game variation:** Give participants a cone which they have to hit the ball over.
- **Game variation:** Participants work with a partner to keep the rally going. One partner stands on each side of the line they are working over.

Net Champ AGES **8-16**

EQUIPMENT

One tennis ball between two, one tennis racket each, one tennis court per four participants.

GAME

Use this activity to develop net play. Each participant should be given a racket and arranged into pairs. Each pair gets one ball and works on half a court. Participants should stand on opposite sides of the net, on the service line. A game is played using the usual rules and scoring system. The difference in this game is that the court is reduced in length, so participants can work on shots played at the net. The service line replaces the baseline as the back of the court. Thus if a tennis ball lands on the floor past the service line it is deemed out, and the participant hitting the shot loses the point. The tennis ball is served by throwing it underarm. The receiver must allow it to bounce before returning it for the first time.

> **Safety Tips**
>
> ▸ Participants need to be careful of other players working on the court next to them. If there is doubt that they would hit another player, they should call 'let' and play the point again.
>
> ▸ Warn participants to be careful of collisions when retrieving stray tennis balls.

ADVICE

- Participants who move in to the net trying to play volley shots win more points. They should only do this if they have their opponent on the defensive.

- Instruct the participants to return to the ready position after each shot.

VARIATIONS

- **Badminton:** This game can be played in badminton sessions. Obviously the shuttlecock cannot bounce after the service, but the rest of the rules are the same.
- **Doubles:** Play the same game as doubles, using the full width of the court.
- **Game variation:** Start with a 'cooperative rally' of three or five shots to give the participants more practice.
- **Large groups:** Use *Champ of the Court* rules (page 168) or *Three in a Row* rules (page 182) if you have more than two participants per half a court.

React   AGES **5-16**

EQUIPMENT

One tennis ball each.

GAME

Use this activity to develop quick reactive movements, which are essential for success in tennis. The set-up of this activity is shown in figure 8.5. Arrange the participants into pairs, then give one of each pair two tennis balls. Ask participants to face their partner, standing 2 to 5 m apart. The participant with the tennis balls holds one in each hand and lifts his or her arms out sideways at shoulder height, then drops one of the tennis balls to the ground. Partners have to react quickly and attempt to catch the ball with one hand before it bounces twice on the floor. Catchers should have five attempts before switching roles with the droppers.

> ### Safety Tips
>
> ▶ Ensure the participants are not working too close to other pairs.
> ▶ Warn participants to be careful of collisions.
> ▶ Participants reacting should stay on their feet at all times. Instruct them not to dive to catch the ball.

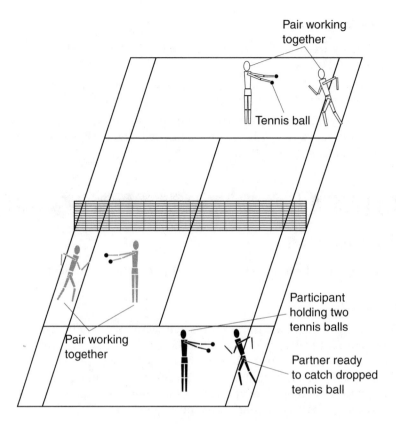

Figure 8.5

⬤ *ADVICE*

- Tennis balls must have adequate bounce. Old tennis balls that have lost some of their springiness should not be used.
- This activity can only be carried out on harder or bouncier surfaces.
- Participants who have limited catching skills can be allowed to catch the ball with two hands.
- Alter the distance between partners depending on age and ability. A bigger gap should make catching the tennis ball more difficult.

VARIATIONS

- **Game variation:** Participants catch the ball on a racket instead of in their hands.
- **Game variation:** Make the game into a competition, counting how many catches each participant gets in a set time.
- **Sport-specific:** This game can be adapted for use in other sports that require reactive catching (e.g., basketball and netball) by dropping the relevant type of ball.

 **Shadow Play** AGES **5-16**

EQUIPMENT

One tennis racket each, one tennis court per eight participants.

GAME

Use this activity as part of a progressive warm-up. It helps to develop movement patterns and footwork techniques. Arrange the participants into groups of no more than eight, with each group working on a different tennis court. Give participants a tennis racket each and instruct them to move around the tennis court carrying out your commands. The following are some of the commands you could give:

- Directions—forwards, backwards, right or left
- Ready position—participants assume this position imagining an opponent is about to play a shot back to them
- Specific shots—smash, volley backhand, volley forehand and so on

Safety Tips

▶ Warn participants to be aware of others when swinging their rackets.

▶ Don't have too many participants on one court.

▶ Warn participants to be careful of collisions.

● *ADVICE*

- If using this activity as part of a warm-up, make sure the movements are progressive. Increase the intensity and speed of movements as the warm-up develops.
- Look for participants using correct footwork techniques.

● *VARIATIONS*

- **Badminton:** This game can be played in badminton sessions using the same rules but modifying the call to badminton shots.
- **Small groups:** With smaller groups, participants can work with a partner on one court per pair. They can tell each other where they have 'hit' an imaginary tennis ball or what shot they have played so that their partner has to play a suitable shot in return.
- **Small groups:** With smaller groups, participants can work on their side of a court. Shout out an area of the court where the participants must move to. When they get there they should choose an appropriate shot to play, then return to the centre of the court. For example, call 'front' and participants move in to play a smash or volley shot.

Team Rally   AGES 8-16

● *EQUIPMENT*

One tennis ball and tennis court per 10 to 12 participants, one tennis racket each.

● *GAME*

Use this activity as part of a progressive warm-up and to develop a range of different tennis strokes. The set-up is shown in figure 8.6. Arrange the participants into groups of 10 to 12, each group working on their own court. Groups should be organised into two lines of five, one line standing behind each of the baselines. The front participant in one of the lines gets a tennis ball and serves it across the net to the front person in the opposite line. After playing a shot participants must run off the court to the right, run round the net to the opposite baseline and join the back

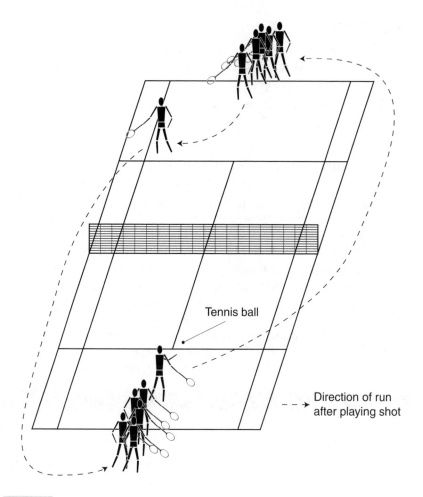

Tennis ball

Direction of run
after playing shot

Figure 8.6

of the other line. Participants must work cooperatively to keep the rally going for as long as possible. A point is scored for every shot played. If the rally breaks down or any rules are broken (e.g., the tennis ball bounces twice before a participant strikes the ball), the rally should be started again with the score starting from zero. Groups compete against each other and the one with the highest-scoring rally at the end of a specified time (e.g., 5 minutes) wins the game.

Safety Tips

▶ If you have more than one court working, and the gap between the courts is small, players on one court should run left while those on the next court run right.

▶ Ensure the participants waiting in line stand well back from the baseline.

▶ Ensure participants who have played their shot move quickly out of the way to allow the next player into position. They should also take regular glances at the play as they are moving round the court to avoid being hit by stray shots.

▶ If it is not possible to run round the side of the net safely, participants should touch one of the sidelines before returning to the back of the same queue.

ADVICE

• Tell the players to work cooperatively to keep the rally going.

• Ask the participants to count out loud the number of shots they have had in each rally to know how many shots their group has had as they play.

• The game can be adapted for working on specific shots. For example, participants must attempt to play forehand ground strokes, or start closer to the net and play volley shots.

VARIATIONS

• **Badminton:** This game can be played in badminton sessions using the same set-up but with relevant rules; for example, the shuttlecock is not allowed to bounce.

• **Game variation:** Each participant carries a tennis ball. If the rally breaks down, the participant who was due to play the next shot can serve a ball straight away. This should get the next rally started quickly. Servers should retrieve the last tennis ball played before joining the back of the line. If collecting the ball is likely to interrupt other participants, the ball should be collected before the rally is started.

- **Harder:** After the rally has continued for 10 shots, participants can try to win a point by playing a shot that cannot be returned by the next hitter. Count up the number of points scored by each participant. The player who has scored the most points at the end of a set time (e.g., 5 minutes) wins the game.
- **Harder:** For more advanced players, having smaller numbers in each group means they have to work harder.
- **Table tennis:** The game can also be played in table tennis sessions using the same set-up and rules.

Three in a Row

AGES **8-16**

EQUIPMENT

One tennis racket each, one tennis ball and tennis court per six participants.

GAME

Having more than four players per court can be a major problem, with participants having to wait a long time for a game. *Three in a Row* can accommodate more people per court and can be used to develop most tennis shots. Arrange the participants into groups of six, with each group working on one court. Separate the groups into two teams of three. The teams stand behind the baseline on opposite sides of the net, one player behind the other (see figure 8.7). The first participant in each line walks onto court to play a point out. The participant who wins the point stays on court to face the next opponent. The losing participant moves to the back of his or her line, allowing the next team-mate onto court. The participant who wins this point attempts to win three points in a row, thereby beating all of the other team. If this is achieved, a game is won and the next participant from both teams moves up for the next point. Play until one team has won a set number of games (e.g., three to five) or for a set time (e.g., 5 to 10 minutes).

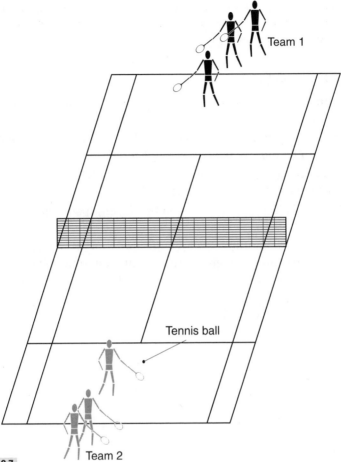

Team 1

Tennis ball

Figure 8.7

Team 2

Safety Tips

▸ Ensure the participants waiting for their turn are out of the way of those playing. This should reduce the chances of them being hit by a racket or tennis ball.

▸ Participants waiting in line must keep their eye on play so that they are not hit by any shots that get past their team-mate on court.

● *ADVICE*

• This game is good for sessions where you have large numbers of participants but only a few tennis courts.

- It can be adapted for working on specific shots. For example, participants must attempt to play forehand ground strokes, or start closer to the net and play volley shots.

✸ VARIATIONS

- **Badminton:** The game can be played in badminton sessions using the same rules.
- **Doubles:** Doubles can be played using the same rules. Obviously this should only be played on a full court.
- **Game variation:** Start with a 'cooperative rally' of three or five shots to give the participants more practice.
- **Harder:** Points can only be won by playing specific shots, such as a volley.
- **Harder:** Use conditioned areas of the court to develop specific shots. An example might be to use only the front half of the court to develop net play (similar to *Net Champ,* page 175).
- **Large groups:** Larger groups can be accommodated by having six participants per half a court.

About the Authors

Anthony Dowson has over 12 years' coaching experience and was previously Head of A-level Physical Education at Ryton Comprehensive School and Loughborough College. He is a qualified coach educator and has assessed a number of coaches in England who have travelled to the States to work for Major League Soccer Camps.

Keith E.J. Morris is the owner of Grass Roots, a successful coaching company and the largest of its kind in northeast England. Grass Roots organises coaching and activity weeks for children, promoting participation in sport and helping to foster healthy lifestyles. Each year the company delivers courses to more than 10,000 children. Keith has a background in education and previously worked as the Head of PE at Corbridge Middle School.